THE TWELVE IMMUTABLE LAWS OF HUMOR

By Billy Riggs

*Featuring 100 of the
World's Greatest Jokes!*

The Twelve Immutable Laws of Humor

Published by
Executive Books
206 West Allen Street
Mechanicsburg, PA 17055
717-766-9499   800-233-2665
Fax: 717-766-6565
www.executivebooks.com

ISBN: 0-937539-52-X

LCCN: 00-108228

Printed in the United States of America

2000

Second printing: 2001

Dedicated to my father,

Bill Riggs, Sr.,

who taught me to laugh.

4

TABLE OF CONTENTS

.

INTRODUCTION

A guy is in town visiting his college buddy, who takes him to a nearby pub. As they sit drinking, the visitor hears one of the locals shout a number, and everyone in the bar cracks up. He says, "What's going on?" So his friend tells him that everyone in town has known everyone else for so long that they've memorized each other's jokes and assigned each a number. That way, they can save time by just shouting the number instead of telling the whole story again. He says, "Observe." He clears his throat and shouts, "Twenty-two!" and all of the guys fall off their chairs laughing. The visitor says, "That's amazing. Let me try." So he yells as loudly as he can, "Nineteen!" But he is met with dead silence. There's not a smile in the house. He says to his buddy, "What did I do wrong?" The friend says, "WELL, YOU KNOW, SOME PEOPLE CAN TELL 'EM AND SOME PEOPLE CAN'T!"

I wish I had a dollar for each time someone has told me, "I just can't tell jokes like you can, Billy." So I've written a book not only to provide the humor-impaired with what I believe to be the best jokes on earth, but to explain how to tell them effectively. I'll never forget the first time I attempted to tell a joke while speaking publicly. No one laughed. I was stunned, because I had heard that very joke told by a public speaker only a few weeks before and watched paramedics carry three guys out on stretchers! Obviously the problem was not with the story, but with the way I had told it. I determined then and there to make a life-long study of what makes people funny, a study that has led me to conclude that there are twelve unchanging rules of humor. They applied as inexorably to Shakespeare as they do to Robin Williams. If you follow these rules, you will be funny. If you don't, you won't. Fortunately, humor is not reserved for those with an innate talent for comedy. While some people obey the twelve immutable laws instinctively, this does not prevent those who lack this natural ability from learning them and applying them equally well. To prove my point I should mention that I've since told that same joke (the one that initially bombed) dozens of times, and now my audiences find it hilarious.

I'm also convinced that jokes can be some of the best teachers on earth, if the story-teller knows how to exploit them. This is because humor always contains an element of truth, or at least a bad example from which to learn. All of the witty stories in this book are what I call "franchise jokes," because an entire speech or lesson can be built around the lessons they teach, much as an NBA team can be built around a franchise player like Michael Jordan. I've frequently given talks in which a key sentence from the opening joke is repeated several times throughout the talk, driving home the powerful point it conceals.

The key to building a message on a funny story is mastering the transition statement that follows the punch line. In order to help the speakers, ministers, and teachers who will use this little volume, I've included an example of at least one transition line following each entry.

LAW ONE

The Law of Abandonment

It was every young speaker's worst nightmare. I was giving my first public speech, opening with the obligatory extraneous joke. I'll never forget delivering the punch line, and hearing that spontaneous burst of... silence. No one laughed. Even two teenagers in the back row who had been giggling throughout the meeting at their own private conversation *stopped* laughing! Everyone stared, some having no clue that I had even attempted to make them laugh, others quietly empathizing with my embarrassing plight. I later realized that my joke had bombed terribly, not because it was a bad joke (it's actually a great one, and it's in this book), but because I had unknowingly violated the first law of humor.

I told that story as though I was not certain that it was particularly humorous, in order that I might somehow save face if the story fell flat. I, like all unseasoned speakers, reasoned unconsciously that if the audience didn't think my story was funny, they would at least credit me with the good sense to *know* that it wasn't funny. It seemed reasonable that I could limit the damage to my ego in this way. After all, it is certainly better to be considered merely humorless, than humorless *and dumb*, as well. Regrettably, this tactic never works.

When a story is told with reservation, those in the audience don't laugh. On the contrary, they wonder why the speaker bothered to tell the story in the first place. The sharks can smell the speaker's fear a mile away, and they perceive him or her as under-confident and timid, as well as humorless and not-too-bright. For this reason, the law of abandonment is crucial. It is the most potent weapon in the speaker's arsenal, a Patriot Missile guaranteed to intercept his or her next bomb.

The law of abandonment can be compared to deliberately climbing out on a limb and sawing it off. When telling a joke, you must commit yourself to it with reckless abandon, never entertaining a thought that the joke might fail to evoke hysterical laughter. If the audience thinks you're not absolutely sure your story will make everyone laugh, they probably won't even crack a smile, for two reasons.

First, most people are self-conscious. Consequently, if you don't communicate non-verbally that your story will make everyone laugh, each person will fear the embarrassment of being the *only one* laughing. Therefore, each will choose not to be the first to laugh. And, of course, if no one is willing to be the first, no one will be second, either. Communicating through your demeanor that your story will result in an instantaneous burst of laughter reassures the audience that there is no danger of embarrassment.

The second reason people fail to laugh when the law of abandonment is violated is this: most people are fundamentally polite, and will be reticent to laugh at your story for fear of hurting *your* feelings. You see, if the audience is not certain that you believe your story is funny, they won't laugh - just in case the story is intended as a serious one. For example, if you were to tell an audience in deadpan fashion that you fell down the steps in front of your house, people would have no way of knowing whether to laugh at your clumsiness or empathize with your pain. The audience fears that if they burst out laughing, you might well follow with a sentence like: "I broke my leg in three places." The audience has to be certain that you're trying to tell a funny story or, in fear that you might intend it as a serious one, they will choose the safe bet: quiet empathy and compassion.

So how do you communicate to your audience that your story is intended to evoke laughter instead of sympathy? One way would be to use the standard old line, "A funny thing happened to me the other day..., or I heard a great joke last week...." However, this is a very amateurish and unnecessary approach.

The best way to inform the listener that your tumble down the steps was comical, not tragic, is through non-verbal communication. So when telling a funny story, smile, change your cadence, exaggerate your facial expressions, tell your story in "joke format", etc. When you're trying to be funny, be very funny. When you're telling a serious story, be very serious. Otherwise, your audience won't know how to respond, and they will sit stone-faced in response to even the funniest of stories. Make sure that your audience knows for certain that you are telling what you believe to be a hilarious story. This is the law of abandonment.

EXAMPLE #1: THE LAW OF ABANDONMENT

Following is a joke for which this law is even more critical than normal. This is because the punch line requires a moment's thought on the part of the audience before they "get it." When you use this type of story, you should use every device imaginable to communicate that it is a funny story, and the audience will laugh. Tell it with reservation, however, and it won't even merit a groan.

The story goes that a group of Ostriches were playing in a field one day, when they heard some rustling in the nearby brush. Sensing immediate danger, the leader of the flock shouted, "Quick, everyone hide!" And so they did - they all buried their heads in the sand! Well, as things turned out, the noise was just another ostrich, who emerged from the brush, looked around at all of his friends with their heads in the sand, and said, "Hey! WHERE IS EVERYBODY?"

I wish I had a dollar for everyone I know who handles problems this way.

EXAMPLE #2: THE LAW OF ABANDONMENT

This particular story is the quintessential example of the need for abandonment in story-telling. It requires confidence, showmanship, and a total lack of inhibition.

The Assistant Priest of a Catholic Church was struggling internally with the low level of his pay. He decided upon a means of communicating his dissatisfaction with the congregation - he walked to the pulpit on Sunday morning and sang: [sing this in Gregorian chant style] "I am the assistant priest of this church. I make only four hundred dollars a week. This is not enough." Well, the Senior Priest heard this, and thought it might help him, too. When his turn at the pulpit came, he walked forward and sang: [again, sing Gregorian chant style] "I am the Senior Priest of this church. I make only five hundred dollars a week. This is not enough." With that, the organist stood up, and walked to the pulpit. Gently nudging the priest aside, he sang: [Sing Gregorian Chant style] "I am the organist of this church. I make eight hundred dollars a week. [At this point, break into a smile and start singing the Broadway show tune:] AND THERE'S NO BUSINESS LIKE SHOW BUSINESS, LIKE NO BUSINESS I KNOW!"

Well, now you know why I'm in show business....

EXAMPLE #3: THE LAW OF ABANDONMENT

The key to making the following story work well is to go out on a limb and saw it off. Unless told wholeheartedly, it will result in a groan instead of laughter.

A man was driving his taxicab down the road one day, and found himself behind an eighteen-wheeler at a traffic light. While the light was red, the truck driver jumped out with a 2x4 in his hand and ran completely around the truck beating on it with all of his might. He then hopped back in the truck and drove off when the light turned green. The cab stayed right behind him. At the next traffic light, the trucker again jumped out and ran around the truck beating on it with a 2x4. This happened at the next three lights, and finally the cab driver couldn't contain his curiosity any more. He waited for the next traffic light, and when the trucker jumped out with his 2x4, the cab driver got out and stopped the guy. He said, "Look buddy, for the last fifteen minutes I've been watching you beat on this truck at every red light. Why are you doing this?" Still banging on the trailer, the trucker shouted, "Well, there's a ten ton load limit on this truck, AND I'VE GOT TWENTY TONS OF CANARIES BACK HERE SO I HAVE TO KEEP HALF OF THEM FLYING ALL THE TIME!"

Life gets so hectic sometimes that you feel like a guy running around beating on a truck every three minutes, don't you?

EXAMPLE #4: THE LAW OF ABANDONMENT

A first-grade teacher gave an assignment to her students. She told them to draw a picture of someone very special to them. So the students took out their crayons and busily set to work. The teacher wandered through the classroom observing the students, offering advice and giving encouragement. Then she came to one little girl, looked at what she was drawing, and a puzzled expression came over her face. She couldn't figure out who this little girl was trying to draw. She said, "Susie, that's a very interesting portrait. Who are you drawing?" Susie kept on coloring as she responded, "I'm drawing a picture of God." The teacher looked surprised and said, "Susie, you can't draw a picture of God. No one knows what He looks like!" Not even looking up from her portrait, Susie said, "THEY WILL WHEN I GET THROUGH!"

Have you ever wondered what God is like? The Bible makes the answer clear. He is exactly like Jesus.

EXAMPLE #5: THE LAW OF ABANDONMENT

There was once a young man who decided to try to economize. So instead of taking the bus home as he usually did, he waited for the bus, and then jogged home behind it, getting some exercise and saving bus fare all at the same time. He arrived home dripping with sweat. He strode proudly into the house and announced to his wife: "Honey, I want you to know that I just jogged home behind the bus and saved 75 cents!" His wife, to his surprise, shook her head in disgust. She said, "You are so dumb." He said, "What do you mean?" She said, "You must be the dumbest man who ever lived. Think about it. You jogged home behind a bus and saved 75 cents. With the same amount of effort, YOU COULD HAVE JOGGED HOME BEHIND A TAXI AND SAVED EIGHT DOLLARS!"

That's what we call creative accounting. Unfortunately, it seems to be what the federal government calls business as usual.

EXAMPLE #6: THE LAW OF ABANDONMENT

There was once a little boy who was an eternal optimist, so much so that it worried his father. The father decided to take advantage of the boy's tenth birthday to teach him a hard lesson in realism. For the boy's birthday, the father bought a piano crate, filled it to the top with manure, and gift-wrapped it. The birthday arrived, and the little boy tore the paper off with glee. He pried the lid off, saw the manure, and looked puzzled for a moment. Then his eyes lit up and he jumped in head first and began thrashing around in it. The father couldn't believe it. He said, "Son, what in the world are you doing?" The little boy, still digging around in the manure said, "THERE'S GOT TO BE A PONY IN HERE SOMEWHERE!"

Now, I know that we seem to be about neck deep in manure right now, but I'm convinced that there's a pony in here somewhere.

13

EXAMPLE #7: THE LAW OF ABANDONMENT

Three science professors, each from a different university, attended a symposium together. During a break they began to boast about their university's aerospace research programs. The first was from (name a university in your area). He said: "My university is studying the feasibility of a mission to Mars." The second was from (name a different university). He said: "That is nothing, my friend. My university is helping NASA plan a mission to Venus." The third was from [Fill in the name of a university you want to pick on.]. Not to be outdone, he boasted. "That's nothing. My university is laying the groundwork for a manned flight to the Sun!" The other two rolled their eyes and said, "You idiot, you can't go to the sun. You'd be burned to a cinder!" The professor replied, "We have developed a solution to that problem. We're going to land... AT NIGHT!"

That's about the level of thinking that I believe is being used by our competition when they state that...

LAW TWO

The Law of Inflation

Nothing is worse than telling a joke and hearing nothing but crickets chirping in response. But a collective groan is almost as bad. When a joke evokes a groan it is usually the result of one of three causes:

1. It's not funny.
2. The law of abandonment was violated.
3. The law of inflation was violated.

This chapter will tell you how to evoke laughter from jokes that on the lips of others produce only groans. The key is the law of inflation.

Telling a joke can be compared to blowing up a balloon slowly, then deliberately popping it. It is essential that the balloon enlarge gradually, not suddenly, and that it be popped suddenly, not gradually. The proper telling of a joke creates tension in an audience, much the way air forced into a balloon stretches and stresses the rubber. Laughter is the sudden release of this pressure. If the "balloon" has not been inflated sufficiently, it cannot be popped successfully. Furthermore, the greater the tension, the more powerful the pop. For this reason, each story must be told carefully, gradually increasing the audience's anticipation of the punch line to its optimum level. If done properly, the audience will laugh even if the joke is not particularly funny!

Another helpful illustration might be that of a water glass, being slowly filled almost to the top so that an overflow is made possible by only a small amount of added water. The manner in which a joke is told should be seen as a means of slowly filling the audience's "giggle box" so that when the punch line is delivered, even a moderately humorous story produces an overflow of guffaws.

All naturally funny people know that blowing up the comedy balloon usually requires exactly three "breaths;" rarely will two suffice, and generally four will be overkill. This is why there are usually three men sitting in a bar or three old ladies knitting, etc. in any joke. Why not two? Why not four? Why does a joke involve a Jew, and Chinaman, and a Greek? Why not just the first two? Why not add a Scotsman for good measure? It's because experience has taught every funny person that three is generally funnier than two or four. Three parts to your joke will usually build the precise amount of tension desired. Two will generally not produce enough tension to pop the balloon, but four sometimes gives the "rubber" too much time to adjust to the pressure, detracting from the power of the "pop," the punch line.

Tension is built in several ways. The first is to apply law number one fully. Tell your story with such complete abandon that the audience will eagerly anticipate the punch line of what they assume must be a hilarious joke. Acting as though you are resisting the impulse to burst out laughing as you tell the story is a powerful tension builder, and the thoroughness with which you sell the punch line before it is ever delivered will dictate in large measure the intensity of the laughs it generates.

Another way to build tension is to create within the story a progression - a progression of danger, or absurdity, or severity of consequences, or intensity of frustration, etc. Almost any progression will suffice, as each step in the sequence will add more tension to the balloon. The first example below contains an ever-increasing degree of boldness on the part of a burglar. As his daring increases, so does the audience's anticipation of the punch line

EXAMPLE #8: THE LAW OF INFLATION

A small-time burglar was planning a break-in. He had been casing a particular house for days, and knew the home was empty. Under cover of darkness, he jimmied a window, hopped up on the window sill and put one foot on the living room floor. That's when he saw in the far corner something he had not bargained for: the biggest, blackest, meanest Doberman Pincer he had ever laid eyes on. The dog growled ominously, but remained motionless. A few minutes later, the thief dared to put his other foot on the floor to see how the dog would respond. The Doberman stayed put, but the thief heard a voice from above. It said: "You'll be sorry." Looking up, the crook saw that the voice was that of a parrot in a cage. Eventually, the thief became bold enough to stand up.

The dog remained in place, and the parrot repeated his warning: "You'll be sorry." The thief then went into the kitchen and stole the silverware. The parrot said: "You'll be sorry." The crook went to the bedroom and stole the jewelry, and the parrot said: "You'll be sorry." Returning to the living room, the crook pushed the TV out the window. As he sat on the window sill to leave, he looked at the dog, still sitting motionless on the floor, and laughed. The parrot said: "You'll be sorry." Exasperated by now, the burglar looked up and said, "You stupid parrot, is that all you can say? 'You'll be sorry?'" The parrot looked back and said: "No.... SIC 'EM!"

Now this thief made a big mistake: he ignored repeated warnings until it was too late. A lot of us make a similar mistake in our businesses [or spiritual lives, or families, etc.].

EXAMPLE #9: THE LAW OF INFLATION

This next story becomes funnier and funnier because of the increasing fury of the mechanic and the simultaneous growing hysteria of Mr. Jones. This double-dose progression yields huge laughs from a story that would otherwise merit only a few chuckles or a groan.

I'd like to tell you about a guy named Jones. Jones owned a Ford Pinto, and whenever it broke down, he took it to the same service station to be worked on by a mechanic named Bubba. Now, Jones was an irritating sort of guy. He never paid attention to the big white line on the pavement - the white line that the customers aren't supposed to cross. Jones never stayed behind the white line. He stood over the mechanic's shoulder watching, talking, questioning. Well, one day Bubba had had a bad day. And while Jones was pestering him about his car, something in the mechanic's mind just snapped. He wheeled around, grabbed Jones by the throat, pushed him to the far side of the white line, and said, "Jones, let's play a game." Jones said with a smile, "Okay." Bubba said, "Jones, I'll bet you can't stand on that side of the white line while I work on your car." Jones said, "I'll bet I can." So Bubba went back to the car, but instead of working on it, he picked up a sledge hammer and pretended that he was going to hit it. He looked over at Jones, thinking that he would be worried. But Jones was actually standing on the far side of the white line with a smirk on his face. This made the mechanic mad. So he did, indeed, use that sledge hammer to make a huge dent in the hood of Jones' Pinto. He figured Jones would be ticked off. But Jones was actually standing on the far side of the line giggling. This made the mechanic

17

really mad. He used that sledge hammer to bash in the front windshield, the back windshield, and all four windows. He assumed that by now Jones would be furious. But Jones was standing on the other side of the white line laughing so hard he was holding his sides! Now the mechanic was boiling. He took that sledge hammer and pounded Jones' Pinto into a four inch plane off the ground. He spun around, thinking surely Jones would be beside himself with rage. But by now, Jones was laughing so hard, he had actually fallen down on the other side of the white line and was laughing uncontrollably. The mechanic had had it. He walked over, grabbed Jones by the collar, and lifted him high in the air. He shouted, "Jones, what's the matter with you! I've just destroyed your car, and you're over here laughing your fool head off!" And Jones said, "Well, while you were beating up on my car... I STEPPED OVER THE LINE THREE TIMES!"

Now, Jones had a problem. He was playing a game while something really serious was going on. And a lot of you are doing the same thing.

EXAMPLE #10: THE LAW OF INFLATION

The following example employs the progression of hysteria in a faith-healing service as its means of building tension. The more the story-teller hypes the building frenzy within the congregation, the greater the hilarity of the joke.

There was once a faith healer who traveled from town to town conducting healing services. One night, he walked out into the crowd and sauntered up to a man with crutches. He said, "Boy, what's your name?" The man replied that his name was Roger. The healer shouted, "Roger, God is going to heal your legs today! Go up there on stage and stand behind that curtain." The congregation began to shout with anticipation. The healer walked up to another man and said, "What's your name?" The man's wife replied, "His name is John, but he can't speak nary a lick." The faith healer screamed, "John, the Lord is going to loose your tongue today! Go up there and stand behind the curtain with Roger!" The crowd started dancing in the aisles. The faith healer shouted, "Roger, can you hear me?" "Yes" came the reply from behind the curtain. "Then throw out your left crutch." The crutch sailed over the curtain and landed on the floor with a thud. The congregation began to swing from the chandeliers. The healer said, "Roger, throw out your right crutch!" The second crutch landed with a thud in front of the curtain. Pandemonium began to break out. The healer shouted, "John, the Lord has just loosed your tongue! I want you to speak to us. Shout out the first thing that comes to your mind." And after a moment, came John's first words of his life. In a clear voice he shouted, "ROGER FELL DOWN!"

Why is it that God heals some people, and He doesn't heal others?

EXAMPLE #11: THE LAW OF INFLATION

There was once a lumberjack who was getting tired of cutting wood the old fashioned way. He was doing it the way he always had - with a bow saw - and getting pretty fed up with it, too. A whole day's work netted him only about a cord and a half of wood. Finally, he broke down and went to the local hardware store to purchase a chain saw. The salesman assured him that he could cut eight cords of wood each day with it. Well, he went home and the next morning started sawing. But by day's end, he had only cut a quarter of a cord of wood. He decided maybe he wasn't trying hard enough, so the next day he worked harder, and got about a cord of wood. The next day, he began at the crack of dawn and sawed until midnight, netting less than two cords of wood. He was furious. He stomped down to the hardware store and snapped at the salesman: "This thing won't cut even as much as my old hand saw!" The salesman said, "Let me take a look at it." He pulled the cord and it started right up. The lumberjack jumped back and shouted: "WHAT'S THAT NOISE?"

You know, the church is a power tool. Operated apart from the power of God, she's as impotent as a chain saw with the engine off.

OR...

You know, business is a power tool, and the power that makes it work is teamwork....

The aforementioned chain saw joke provides a good illustration of the value of building tension through a progression. The humor of the story is derived not simply from the punch line, but from the increasing determination of the lumberjack to make his chain saw work. If one were to tell the same story, but mention only the lumberjack's first day's work with the chain saw, the logic of the joke would remain substantially unchanged. *But it would not be nearly as funny.* The following example also provides a clear example of the necessity of a progression if one's purpose is to produce laughter. The humor of it lies not only in the outcome, but that the outcome is a frustration of the principal character's tireless and repeated efforts to look younger.

19

EXAMPLE #12: THE LAW OF INFLATION

An 87 year-old bachelor decided that since he was getting along in years, he should try to get in shape, so he walked a quarter of a mile each day. He got himself looking like a 60 or 65 year-old man. One day he saw a friend on the street and shouted, "Hey, Paul, how ya' doing?" The guy looked at him with amazement and said, "Joe Smith?!? Is that you? You look great. Why I never would have recognized you!" This got the bachelor pumped up, so he started jogging a couple of miles a day. He ran into another friend, who said, "Joe Smith?!? Is that you? Why, you look like a 50 year-old man!" Now Joe was really fired up. He started biking, swimming, and running, and before long he had the body of a 30 year-old. In fact, he started dating a 25 year-old woman. They were in a park one day and he decided for the first time in his life to pop the question. She said "Yes", and he was elated. He said, "Wait here and I'll run across the street to get some champagne so we can celebrate." He jumped up, ran into the street and was hit by a truck and killed. A moment later he appeared before the Lord. He immediately began to complain. He said, "Lord, I'm 87 years old. I've never been married. I worked hard to develop the body of a 30 year-old. Now I propose to a 25 year-old woman and she says yes, and then I get hit by a truck and die. Lord, why?" And the Lord looked at him and said: "JOE SMITH?!?"

Sometimes, it seems that your hard work just doesn't pay off, doesn't it? Well, I'm convinced that if we keep it up long enough that one day we'll inevitably hit pay dirt.

EXAMPLE #13: THE LAW OF INFLATION

Yet another means of blowing up the balloon is to tell jokes that contain curious or funny behavior on the part of the participants. This is why talking animal jokes are so often humorous. It is not only *what* the dog says that is so funny, but the mere fact that the dog talks at all. The very idea of a talking dog is enough to evoke smiles from your audience, moving them that much closer to an outright belly-laugh once the punch line is delivered.

A man walked into the office of a talent agent with his little dog behind him. He said, "Sir, I have an act that you won't believe. This is the smartest dog in the world. He can answer any question I throw at him." The agent nodded for him to continue. The man said, "Fido, what do we have over our heads right now?" Fido said, "Roof! Roof!" The agent looked at the man suspiciously. The man continued, "Fido, how does sandpaper feel?" Fido replied, "Ruff! Ruff!" The agent rubbed his temples in disbelief. The man asked again: "Fido, who is the greatest baseball player who ever lived?" Fido responded, "Ruth! Ruth!" Well, the agent had heard enough. He called security and had the man and his dog thrown out into the street. As the man brushed off his clothes, the dog shook his head and snapped with disgust, "I KNOW, I KNOW, I SHOULD HAVE SAID DIMAGGIO."

The moral of this story is this: always lead with your best stuff. That's what I intend to do here tonight.

EXAMPLE #14: THE LAW OF INFLATION

A wonderful little story about a small town flood employs the curious behavior of a hat in order to build tension, evoke smiles, and prepare the audience for laughter.

The story goes that there was flood in a small town. A man was swept up in the waters, and finally managed to work his way toward a house and climb up on the roof. He sat down next to a woman who was perched atop that same roof. As they sat there, the man noticed a baseball cap floating by the front of the house. To his surprise, when it got about ten feet past the end of the house, it turned around and began to float against the current. And when it passed the house by about ten feet on that side, it turned around and floated back the other way. The cap made several cycles like this, back and forth in front of the house, baffling the man so thoroughly that he just had to ask about it. He turned to the woman and said: "Do you have any idea what could be making that hat do that?" She said, "I sure do. That's my husband under there." She added: "HE PROMISED ME HE'D MOW THE LAWN TODAY COME HELL OR HIGH WATER!"

Don't you love a person who sticks to his word? The guy that makes a promise and fulfills it come hell or high water?

EXAMPLE #15: THE LAW OF INFLATION

I once heard author and speaker Charlie "Tremendous" Jones deliver the following joke that uses an unusual manner of speech as the means of preparing the audience for laughter.

There was a coup in a small African nation and a new dictator came to power. An American journalist was sent to interview him for television. He said, "Mr. President, what are your plans for the country now that you have assumed power?" The dictator replied, "It is my plan [stop here and whistle, oscillating between high and low pitches] to expand the industrial base [whistle] and increase exports [whistle]. I will consolidate the government [whistle] to cut spending [whistle], thus reducing the national indebtedness [whistle]." The reporter responded, "Mr. President, I am very impressed with your ability to speak English, albeit very unusual. Tell me, where did you learn to speak English?" The dictator replied, "[Whistle] SHORT-WAVE RADIO!"

I guess it's axiomatic that a person's learning will always reflect the quality of the teaching he or she has received.

EXAMPLE #16: THE LAW OF INFLATION

The next story capitalizes on the lengths to which a pet owner goes to get his very expensive parrot to talk. With each item that the owner buys, the audience's anticipation of the outcome builds.

The story goes that a man went to a pet shop to buy a parrot. There were two on display, one for $50, and one for $500. The guy asked the clerk: "Why the difference in price?" The man replied: "Well, the $500 parrot talks like no parrot you've ever heard". The guy says, "I'll take it." He slaps 500 bucks on the table, and walks home with the parrot in a cage. A couple of days later he comes back and says: "Hey, this bird won't talk." The clerk says: "Well, did he climb his little ladder?" The guy says: "What ladder?" The salesman says: "This bird won't talk unless he has a little ladder in his cage." So the guy buys a little ladder for 18 bucks. Two days later he's back. The bird still won't talk. The clerk says: "Did he climb his little ladder?" The guy says "Yeah." "Did he ring his little bell?" The guy says "What bell? He doesn't have a little bell." The clerk says, "He won't talk unless he has a little bell to ring." The guy

pays nine bucks for a little bell and goes home. The next day, he's back.
The bird still won't talk. The clerk says: "Did he climb his little ladder?"
"Yep." "Did he ring his little bell?" "Yep." "Did he look in his little mir-
ror?" The guy says: "What mirror?" The clerk says: "This bird won't talk
unless he can see himself in a little mirror." So the guy pays twelve bucks
for a little mirror. He's back the next day. The bird still won't talk. "Did
he climb his little ladder?" "Yes." "Did he ring his little bell?" "Yes." Did
he look in his little mirror?" "Yes." "Did he swing on his little swing?"
The guy says: "How much for the swing?" He pays fifteen bucks for a
swing. The next day he's back. He says: "The bird is dead." The clerk
says, "That's terrible! Well, did he ever talk before he died?" The guy says,
"Yeah, he did. You'd have been proud of him. He climbed up his little
ladder, he rang his little bell, he looked in his little mirror, he swung on
his little swing, then he fell off. And as he lay there with his little legs
sticking up in the air, he said with his last breath, 'THEY DIDN'T SELL
BIRDSEED?'"

Now, this guy made a big mistake. He bought all of the non-essentials, but overlooked the one key ingredient. I think we have a tendency to do that in business, too.

EXAMPLE #17: THE LAW OF INFLATION

This next story uses the humorous idea of a preacher having to jump off a moving train to avoid missing a preaching assignment. The very idea is funny, and will fill the glass to the brim before the punch line is delivered, resulting in an overflow of laughter. Notice that there are two points in the story that will produce audible laughter before the punch line. This example of multiple punch lines provides a beautiful segue into the next method of inflating the laughter balloon, which is explained in Example #18.

There was once a New York businessman who was invited to
interview for the job of his dreams. The man lived out on Long Island,
and the job interview was in Queens. On the appropriate day, the man
jumped out of bed, dressed to the nines, and boarded the subway for the
long ride into Queens. Along the way, he struck up a conversation with
an employee of the subway system, and remarked that he would be get-
ting off at Flushing Meadow. The employee was startled and said, "Oh
no. This train never stops at Flushing Meadow during rush hour. This
train is the express, and it goes all the way to Manhattan without

23

stopping." *The guy panicked. He knew that there was no way for him to get off the train in Manhattan and then catch another one back to Queens and get there in time for his interview. He begged the employee to talk with the conductor about stopping at Flushing Meadow for just a few seconds. The man disappeared for a few minutes, and returned and told the man: "The conductor says this train never stops at Flushing Meadow during rush hour, and if he were to stop there today he'd lose his job. So he can't stop the train, but he has agreed to slow it down. [If you pause here, the audience will laugh.] So when you see us pulling through the station at Flushing Meadow and feel the train slowing down, pry the doors open and jump. But when you hit the platform, keep running the same direction as the train so that you won't fall down." Well, that's what the guy did. As the train pulled through the station at Flushing Meadow, he felt it slow down. He pried the door open, and jumped. He hit the ground perfectly, and as he was running down the platform, the train sped up and began to pull away. As one of the rear cars passed him, a big husky guy on board saw the man running down the platform and assumed that he was trying to catch the train. So he pried the doors open, reached out and grabbed the guy by the collar and jerked him back on the train! [A pause here will result in more laughter.] The big man looked at the stunned businessman and said, "You don't know how lucky you are! THIS TRAIN NEVER STOPS AT FLUSHING MEADOW DURING RUSH HOUR!"*

My fear in closing this talk is that in the next few weeks you're going to forget all of the principles I've taught you, and allow the force of habit to jerk you right back onto the same old train you were riding before. I hope that won't be the case.

EXAMPLE #18: THE LAW OF INFLATION

A wonderful means of building tension to its maximum level before delivering a punch line is to have several funny lines in the story, each one funnier than the one before. Following are some examples of this principle.

A really shy fellow by the name of Mort decided that in order to overcome his bashfulness he would join Toastmasters, the public speakers' club. They have this procedure in which everyone draws a card out of a hat, and whatever is written on that card is the subject the member must use for a five-minute impromptu speech. When Mort looked at his card, he was horrified to see the word "sex" on it. But he stood up and did a brilliant job, resulting in a standing ovation from the group. When he got home that evening, his wife asked him what he had spoken on that day and, too embarrassed to tell her the truth, he said, "Motorcycling." The next day, she was having coffee with some friends, and one of them remarked how knowledgeable and eloquent Mort had been at Toastmasters that week. She replied, "Are you kidding me? That is a subject he knows absolutely nothing about! [pause for laughter] Why he's only done it twice in his whole life. [pause for more laughter]. The first time he got motion sickness [pause for more laughter]. AND THE SECOND TIME IT BLEW HIS HAT OFF!"

Well, sex is an awkward subject to talk about, isn't it?

EXAMPLE #19: THE LAW OF INFLATION

Following are several more examples of stories with three punch lines.

Three men joined the army, and were about to receive their duty assignments. The first sat down across the desk from an officer who asked, "What were you in civilian life?" The recruit said, "I was a flight attendant." The officer said, "Great. You'll be assigned to a paratroop squad." A second recruit came in as nervous as he could be. He was asked the same question: "What were you in civilian life?" The man stammered, "I was a M-M-M-M-M-M...." The sergeant interrupted: "YOU'RE ON MACHINE GUN DUTY." The next came in and was asked the same question: "What were you in civilian life?" "I was a comedian," he replied. "Wonderful." said the sergeant. "YOU GO TO MILITARY INTELLIGENCE."

Doesn't the government seem at times to be nothing but a joke?

EXAMPLE #20: THE LAW OF INFLATION

An airline pilot lost his watch, and called the nearest tower for the time. The air traffic controller said, "That depends on which airline you're with." "What do you mean?" the pilot inquired. "Well," the controller said, "If you are flying for American Airlines, the time is 1400. If you're flying for TWA, the time is 2:00 p.m. eastern standard time. If you're in a military aircraft, the time is 1900 Zulu." "But what if you're not any of those?" the pilot asked. "Well," the controller continued, "if you're flying for (fill in the name of an airline you don't like), it's Tuesday. If you're flying for (fill in the name of an airline you like even less), it's September. And if you fly for (fill in the name of the airline you like least), THE BIG HAND IS ON THE TWELVE (pause here to let laughter begin, and finish punch line while laughter is in progress) and the little hand is on the two."

So if you're wondering why I was late to this speaking engagement, now you know.

EXAMPLE #21: THE LAW OF INFLATION

A woman went to a lawyer saying that she wanted to leave her husband. He asked, "Do you have grounds?" She replied, "YES, WE HAVE NEARLY THREE ACRES." [Pause for chuckle.] He said, "No ma'am, you don't understand. I mean do you have a grudge?" She said, "We most certainly do. IT'S A TWO CAR GRUDGE." The lawyer tried again: "Maybe I'm not being specific enough. Does your husband beat you up?" The woman said, "No, I GENERALLY GET UP A HALF-HOUR BEFORE HE DOES." By now the lawyer was frustrated. He said: "What I need to know ma'am, is why you want a divorce." "Oh," she said, "That's easy. MY HUSBAND JUST DOESN'T KNOW HOW TO COMMUNICATE."

All of us have a tendency to blame our problems on someone else, don't we?

EXAMPLE #22: THE LAW OF INFLATION

Two men were gazing at the sky one day admiring a flock of geese flying in their usual "V" formation. One said to the other, "Do you know why one side of the V is always longer than the other?" The other replied, "Yeah. IT'S BECAUSE ONE SIDE HAS MORE GEESE THAN THE OTHER." [Pause for a little laughter here.] The first man said, "You're an accountant aren't you?" [Choose whatever profession you want to pick on here.] The second guy said, "Yeah, how'd you know?" The first guy responded, "Because the information you just gave me is completely accurate.... AND ABSOLUTELY USELESS!"

Do you sometimes feel that you are bombarded in your business with information that may or may not be accurate, but it really doesn't matter because it's absolutely useless to you anyway? Is there a way to make such information useful?

EXAMPLE #23: THE LAW OF INFLATION

A business manager was in the process of interviewing many candidates for a single job, so to save time and narrow the number of candidates down, he decided in the initial interview to ask each applicant three questions. The first candidate came in, and the interviewer said, "Sir, I have three questions for you. First, how many days of the week start with the letter T?" The man thought for a moment and said "Two." "That's correct," said the manager, "And what are they?" The man replied "Today and tomorrow." Well, this was not what the manager had anticipated, but he said, "I guess we can accept that answer. Here's the second question: How many seconds are there in year?" Instantly the man answered "Twelve." "Twelve?" the manager said. "How did you arrive at that number?" "Easy," said the man. "The second of January, the second of February, the second of March...." "I see," said the manager. "I guess we can accept that answer, too. Final question: How many "D's" are there in Rudolph the Red Nosed Reindeer"? Now the man was stumped. He concentrated for over twenty minutes, and finally said, "One hundred and ten." "One hundred and ten?!?" the manager exclaimed. "How in the world did you get that answer?" "Easy," said the man. [Sing to the tune of Rudolph the Red Nosed Reindeer:] "D-D-D-D-D-D-D...."

No matter how simple or difficult a question might be, the answer you get will be determined by the frame of reference, the paradigm of the person answering it. Nowhere is this phenomenon more true than in the realm of politics [or religion, etc.].

EXAMPLE #24: THE LAW OF INFLATION

The story goes that a baby bird fell from it's nest on a cold and blustery day. Badly injured and unable to move, the little bird was terrified of freezing to death. Then along came a friendly cow, who decided to do the only thing she could do to help the little creature. She dropped a pile of warm, fresh manure on top of the bird. Well, before long, the little bird

27

was cozy and warm, even if filthy. In fact, the little bird was so happy about being rescued, he began to sing. Well, wouldn't you know it, a cat happened by and heard the little bird singing. Now, this cat was not about to eat a bird covered in manure, but being its natural enemy, he did reach in and pull the little bird out, leaving him exposed to the cold again. A short time later, the little bird died. Now the moral of the story is threefold. First, it's not always your enemies who get you into it. [Pause for laughter.] Second, it's not always your friends who get you out of it. [Pause for laughter.] And third, when you're in it up to here [put your hand up to your neck], FOR HEAVEN'S SAKE, DON'T SING!

It seems to be an axiom of life that your friends get you into a lot more trouble than your enemies ever will.

EXAMPLE #25: THE LAW OF INFLATION

Following are five stories that employ the classic joke format of three elements. Note that in each case, the story would make perfect sense if the second were omitted altogether. However, to do so would not inflate the balloon sufficiently to produce the loud pop desired.

Three criminals were about to be incarcerated in an experimental prison. All three were to serve 30 year sentences, but each was allowed to take into prison any single thing he wanted. The first opted to take a telephone. The second chose to take his wife. The last chose to take 30 years worth of cigarettes. Three decades later, they emerged, and were escorted to a press conference. The first described how he had set up a business over the phone, and said, "Now I'm a millionaire!" The second said that he had enjoyed this time with his wife and said, "Now I have ten kids and eight grandchildren!" The third - the one who had taken thirty years worth of cigarettes into prison with him - stepped up to the microphone and said: [pause] "ANYBODY GOT A MATCH?"

Now, this third guy made a huge mistake. He made a life-shaping decision without carefully thinking through the details. I think a lot of our pain in life is caused by this type of decision making.

28

EXAMPLE #26: THE LAW OF INFLATION

Three college students decided to attend the track and field conference championships in the Cotton Bowl one year. One student was from the University of Texas, one was from SMU, and the third was from Texas A&M. When they arrived, however, they were told that the event was sold out. Undaunted, they decided to try to sneak in. That's when they saw the athletes making their way through a separate entrance. The University of Texas student had an idea. He cut down a sapling, trimmed the branches, and threw it over his shoulder. He walked up to the athlete's entrance and said, "Smith, University of Texas, pole vault." The guard waved him through. The SMU student caught on quickly. He lifted a manhole cover, tucked it under his arm and said, "Johnson, SMU, discus." The guard waved him through. The Texas A&M student saw this transpire and thought, "I can do this." So he went and got a roll of barbed wire, hoisted it to his shoulder and said, "Jones, Texas A&M, FENCING!"

Now, this story is obviously untrue, but it does highlight what I believe to be the two most serious problems in our schools and universities today: the loss of integrity and the poor quality of education.

EXAMPLE #27: THE LAW OF INFLATION

Two men were riding together in a car, when the driver ran a red light. The passenger said, "Do you realize you just ran a light?" The driver said: "Relax. My brother and I always run red lights." The driver ran another red light, turned to the passenger and said, "Relax. My brother and I always run red lights." The passenger was relieved to see that the next light was green, but to his surprise, the driver came to a screeching halt. He turned to the driver and said, "Man what's the matter with you? You run two red lights, and excuse it by saying that you and your brother always run red lights, then you come to a green light and stop! Why is that?" The driver calmly responded: "Well, I have to stop at green lights, BECAUSE I NEVER KNOW WHEN MY BROTHER MIGHT BE COMING DOWN A SIDE STREET!"

You see, obedience to the laws of the land is critical, because the absence of laws is not freedom, it's anarchy. And once you decide not to stop at red lights, you will eventually have no choice but to begin stopping at green lights. That's the way the world works.

29

EXAMPLE #28: THE LAW OF INFLATION

A young man bought himself a new Ferrari, and being a religious sort of a guy he called the local Catholic church and asked the priest if he would bless it. The priest said, "What's a Ferrari?" The man explained that it was a very expensive imported car. The priest shook his head and replied that he wasn't allowed to bless a car. The young man then called the Baptist Church and asked the preacher there if he would bless his Ferrari. The pastor said, "What's a Ferrari?" Patiently, the man explained that the Ferrari was an exquisite Italian car. The pastor explained that he was sorry, but he just couldn't bless a car. Undaunted, the young man drove down to the Unitarian church, and asked the minister there if he would place a blessing on his new Ferrari. The minister's face lit up. He said, "You own a Ferrari?" The young man, said, "So you know what a Ferrari is?" The minister replied, "Do I?!? Motor Trend Car of the year four years running, zero to sixty in less than six seconds! I'll be thrilled to help you, son. But there's just one problem." "What's that?" the young man asked. The minister furrowed his brow and said, "WHAT'S A BLESSING?"

It seems that on every street corner there's another type of church, all with different beliefs. How do you determine which one is right for you?

EXAMPLE #29: THE LAW OF INFLATION

During the French Revolution, three prisoners were brought forth to be guillotined. The first was escorted to the platform, and asked if he had any last requests. He replied, "Yes. I am a very brave man, and to demonstrate my bravery, I would like to be beheaded face up. I want to see the blade coming." His wish was granted, and he was strapped into the guillotine on his back. The rope was cut, and the blade dropped, but jammed halfway down. Under French law, this was regarded as an act of God, so the condemned man was set free. The second man also requested that he be beheaded while looking at the sky. Again, the blade jammed and he was set free. The third man, likewise, requested that he be beheaded face up, and was locked into the guillotine on his back. But just before the executioner cut the rope, the condemned man shouted, "Wait a minute! I THINK I SEE WHY IT STICKS!"

Sometimes it's not good to tell everything you know, is it?

OR...

I think I know what's making our industry stick. But I'm afraid that if I tell you i'll wind up getting my head cut off.

EXAMPLE #30: THE LAW OF INFLATION

The following story demonstrates the principle of inflation for its own sake. The logic of the joke would remain intact if the man had merely said "That's an ugly baby" one time. But this would be insufficient to inflate the balloon. Having him repeat himself adds greater tension, and therefore greater humor.

A lady was flying cross-country holding her new-born baby, when she noticed the man seated next to her was staring at the child. She gave him a dirty stare, and he immediately apologized. He said, "Ma'am forgive me for staring, but I've just got to tell you that is the ugliest baby I've ever seen." The woman was incensed. The man sensed her shock and said, "Ma'am, I'm sorry. I don't mean to offend you, but I'm serious. That's the ugliest baby I've ever seen, and I'm an obstetrician. I've delivered hundreds of babies before, but I've never seen a child that ugly." The woman was furious. She called the flight attendant and said to her, "Madam, this man is the most offensive and insulting person I've ever met. When this plane lands, I'm going to call my lawyer, and I'm going to file suit against him, and I'm going to sue you, and I'm going to sue this airline for millions." The flight attendant immediately tried to smooth things over. She said, "Oh, ma'am, whatever this man said, I'm sure he didn't mean any harm. In fact, I'll have the captain come back here and personally apologize, and I'm sure the airline will give you your money back for this flight. In fact, there's an empty seat up in first class. I'll upgrade you there now, and while we're up there, I'LL SEE IF I CAN FIND A BANANA FOR YOUR MONKEY."

The truth is a little bit hard to accept sometimes, isn't it?

31

LAWS THREE AND FOUR

The Law of Prompting
The Law of Deflation

Believe it or not, an audience will rarely laugh unless the storyteller sub-liminally tells them to do so, and people will usually laugh at a very bad joke if they are cued to do so. In fact, I have often as an experiment delivered such cues to an audience without saying a word, and up to a fourth of the audience laughs, not even knowing why they have done so! Prompting is a skill applied instinctively and often unconsciously by those who are naturally funny, yet it can be easily and quickly learned by those with no innate sense of comedy. How does one prompt the audience to laugh at the appropriate time?

It is accomplished in two ways: first, when you deliver a punch line, you should open your eyes wide and raise your eyebrows as high as possible. Second, you should be sure your hands are above waist level when the heart of the punch line is stated. Sometimes simply turning the palm upward will enhance the effect of this gesture. David Letterman is a marvelous example of someone with a natural talent for comedy. If you watch him closely, you will notice that he keeps such a high level of anticipation in his audience that he can evoke laughter by simply raising an eyebrow and turning his palm upward. He gets huge laughs without even saying a word, because he is a master of the law of prompting. I've treated laws three and four together in this chapter because both must be accomplished simultaneously, and both relate specifically to the delivery of the punch line.

The term *punch* line implies that its delivery must be as swift and unexpected as a Mike Tyson jab to the midriff. No component of a joke is so crucial to its success as the manner in which the closing line is stated. Even if the balloon has been properly inflated, popping it must be accomplished swiftly and decisively. In order to accomplish this, you must recite the punch line precisely, quickly, and smoothly. If you fail in this endeavor, the result will be comparable to releasing the open end of a balloon, causing it to fizzle instead of explode.

Consequently, the punch line should be phrased in the briefest and most direct way possible, and should be rehearsed until it can be told flawlessly. If you tell the story perfectly, but stumble on even one word of the punch line, the world's funniest jokes will prompt no more than a slight chuckle. This is because the stumble somehow creates a slow leak in the balloon in sufficient degree to prevent a pop. As a general rule (all other factors being equal), the shorter the heart of the punch line is, the funnier the story will become. That is why the story of the parrot and the Doberman described earlier is so hilarious; the punch line is totally unexpected, and only two syllables long: "Sic 'em!"

Conversely, a punch line that takes ten seconds to tell, even if delivered flawlessly, will never work, any more than the popping of a balloon can be prolonged. The goal is to simultaneously and instantaneously release all the tension you placed on the balloon while telling the story. For this reason, the best storytellers instinctively divide the last sentence of some jokes into an extraneous portion followed by the critical part of the punch line, which I call its heart. The first portion is made up of any words in the beginning of a long punch line that do not give away the joke. The heart of the punch line begins with the first word that will reveal to astute people how the joke turns out. In order to assist you in this process, the heart (that is, the part to be said suddenly and smoothly) of each punch line in this book is written in ALL UPPER CASE LETTERS. Rehearse these lines word for word. They are time tested and are all winners.

EXAMPLE #31: THE LAWS OF DEFLATION AND PROMPTING

Notice that in the following story, the truly funny portion of the punch line (in all capital letters) comprises only about a third of the last sentence. This indicates that the portion in upper and lower case letters can and should be told in normal cadence and inflection. It is only the portion in all capital letters that must be said quickly, smoothly, with reckless abandon, and with facial and hand cues.

A man suspected that his wife was cheating on him, so he went home unexpectedly in the middle of the day to see if his suspicions were correct. They lived on the 26th floor of an apartment building, and when he opened the door, he heard a commotion in the bedroom. Sure enough, his wife was in bed in a teddy, and a man's clothes were lying on the floor, but there was no one else in the room. He ransacked the apartment, and finally saw a guy hanging off the balcony wearing nothing but boxer shorts and a t-shirt. He went out and pried the guy's hands loose, and the guy fell 26 floors into the bushes. Miraculously, he survived, and stood up to brush himself off. This infuriated the husband, who went to the kitchen, and with almost superhuman strength lifted the refrigerator and dropped it off the balcony right on top of the guy. But the act of lifting the refrigerator was so stressful, that the husband had a heart attack and died.

A moment later, he found himself sitting in a room with two other men and an angel. It was Saint Pete, who said, "Gentlemen, I've been sent to tell you that the three of you have failed to meet our entrance requirements. However, in the interest of compassion, each day we make an exception for the person who died the most tragic death. Tell me your stories."

The husband related how his wife had been having an affair, and he had dropped a refrigerator on the culprit, causing his own fatal heart attack. Saint Pete responded that this was indeed a tragic death.

The second guy said, "Well, I was doing calisthenics on the balcony of my 27th floor apartment, wearing just my gym shorts and a tank top, when I guess I got careless and fell off. I managed to grab the rail of the balcony below me, but then a guy came out and pried my hands loose. I even survived the fall, but then this refrigerator came from nowhere and landed on my head and killed me!" Saint Pete acknowledged that this, too, was a tragic way to die.

Saint Pete turned to the third guy and asked, "And how did you die?" The guy replied. "Well, it's the craziest thing. There I was, minding my own business, HIDING NAKED IN A REFRIGERATOR...."

There's an old saying that goes "You reap what you sow." This guy found out that no one gets away with it. That's why integrity is so important in life.

EXAMPLE #32: THE LAWS OF DEFLATION AND PROMPTING

This next story provides a clear illustration of how carefully the punch line must be dissected into its extraneous and essential components. Using the entire last sentence as the punch line would make it too long and thus ineffective. However, pausing after the words "patrol car" will spoil its effect. This is because the audience will get the joke before you continue the punch line with the words "blue lights still flashing." Consequently, they will have to delay their laughter until you finish speaking, greatly reducing the impact of the pop. Therefore, the experienced joke-teller will divide the punch line into a maximum of two parts (not necessarily *equal* parts), and will tell the second part with no pauses whatever.

A highway patrolman stopped an obviously drunk driver, and administered the standard tests, having him touch his nose, walk a straight line, etc. But while he was ticketing the man, an accident occurred on the other side of the divided highway. The patrolman told the motorist to wait while he assisted with clearing the accident. The drunk saw his chance to escape and took it. He got back in his car and drove home as fast as he could, telling his wife that if anyone inquired about him, she was to say that he had been home in bed with the flu all day. Within the hour two patrolmen were standing at his front door asking to see him. He came to the door in his bathrobe, coughing and wheezing. He swore he'd been in bed sick all day. They apologized for bothering him, and asked if they could take a look at his car. The man opened the garage, and there, inside it, WAS A HIGHWAY PATROL CAR WITH THE BLUE LIGHTS STILL FLASHING!

Now here's a guy who was literally caught red-handed. I think it's time that we as a company [or society, or church, etc.] acknowledge that we have been caught red-handed, too. [Follow by naming the error you want to address.]

EXAMPLE #33: THE LAWS OF DEFLATION AND PROMPTING

In this story, the punch line is composed primarily of a phone number, but long before the entire number is revealed, the punch line is plain to the audience.

Because reading the entire number is pointless, and actually delays, and therefore detracts from the laughter, only the area code should be used to pop the balloon. More specific directions are included in brackets within the joke, itself.

There was once a tycoon who was out of town on business. He called home and the maid answered. He said, "Let me speak to my wife." She stammered: "But I thought she was with you." The guy replied, "What do you mean?" She said, "Well, sir, I hate to tell you this, but she's been upstairs in the bedroom with someone ever since I got here this morning." The guy said, "I can't believe it! She's cheating on me! Well she's not going to get away with it. Let me tell you what I want you to do. I want you to go in the den and look in my desk. You'll find a pistol there. I want you to go upstairs, burst into the room, and kill them both." She said, "I can't do that, I'll go to jail." So the man says, "Look, I am a very wealthy and powerful man. If you do what I ask, I promise that I'll take good care of you. I'll give you a million dollars and make sure that you never get caught, and that you live out the rest of your life in ease." She thought a minute and said, "Okay." She laid the receiver down, and a couple of minutes later the guy hears two gun shots. BLAM! BLAM! The lady comes back to the phone and says, "Well, I don't believe it, but I did it. What should I do with the gun?" He said, "Go out in the back yard and throw it in the lake," to which she responded, "There's no lake in our back yard." He said, "IS THIS AREA CODE (502) [Pause here. The punch line has essentially been delivered, and laughter will erupt here. As they laugh, you can quietly finish reciting the phone number.] 555-1212?"

One of the greatest causes of disaster in life is jumping to conclusions.

EXAMPLE #34: THE LAWS OF DEFLATION AND PROMPTING

Note that the punch line of the following joke is very long, but the heart of the punch line is not. The portion in upper and lower case letters need not be hurried, because it does not in any way give away the punch line.

There was once a city mayor who was driving down the highway when he saw two city employees on a work detail by the road. As he drove by, he noticed that one man would dig a hole, and the other would come right behind him and fill it up. As he looked behind him, he could see scores of such filled-in holes lining the highway. Well, as you can imagine, he was pretty upset. When he got back to city hall, he asked someone to check it out. Before too long, one of his aids came in and said, "I've looked into it, Mayor. It turns out that it's usually a three-man crew, BUT THE GUY WHO PLANTS THE TREES IS OUT SICK TODAY!"

Now, here were two guys working and going through the motions, but all of their efforts were meaningless. I think a lot of businesses could take a lesson from this tree-planting crew.

EXAMPLE #35: THE LAWS OF DEFLATION AND PROMPTING

The following story has a rather long punch line. Therefore, great care must be taken to state it as one long phrase with no pauses. The importance of compressing the punch line in order to ensure that everyone in the audience gets the joke at the same moment (or as nearly the same moment as possible) cannot be over-stressed.

Once there was a very poor man who lived in a little shack. His back porch was falling apart, and he couldn't afford to repair it, so he broke into a local sawmill and stole enough lumber to fix it. Well, he liked the results, and he liked the price even better, so he made a habit of breaking into that sawmill and making off with whatever lumber he could carry. Over the years, he turned that little shack into a veritable mansion. In fact, he became so wealthy that the local Baptist church elected him a deacon. [Opening the eyes wide as you say the word deacon will usually produce a chuckle from the audience.] Well, now the man was in a quandary. He just couldn't see himself accepting the position of church deacon with all of this thieving on his conscience. And he certainly wasn't going to tell _his_ preacher what he had been doing all those years. So he decided to go talk to the priest at the Catholic church where he knew the confessional was confidential. He said, "Father, is it okay if I make my confession to you even though I'm a Baptist?" The priest said, "Certainly, my son." The man began to unburden himself about his life of stealing. Finally, he said, "Thank you, Father. I feel one hundred percent better. I guess now I can go and become a deacon." The priest said, "Wait a minute, son. You can't just come in here and confess and be forgiven. You have to do something to make up for your sins. Tell me something: Have you ever made penance before?" The man thought for a minute and said, "No, [pause] BUT IF YOU HAVE THE PLANS I SURE KNOW WHERE WE CAN GET THE LUMBER TO BUILD ONE!"

You know, some of us never learn from our mistakes....

EXAMPLE #36: THE LAWS OF DEFLATION AND PROMPTING

The following two stories provide a terrific illustration of the simultaneous use of the laws of deflation and prompting. The heart of the punch line (the part in all capital letters) is told not only suddenly and unexpectedly, but with a complete change in facial expression. The humor of the story lies as much in the facial expression and change in tone as it does in the words, themselves.

A guy had a problem with his phone bill, and called the phone company to object. A lady manager spoke with him, and concluded that the bill was accurate, and that the man would have to pay it. The dispute quickly escalated into a heated argument, which ended with the man slamming the receiver down after screaming, "You can just take this phone and shove it!" Well, the lady at the phone company had heard enough. She quickly dispatched two repairmen to go the man's house with orders to remove the phone. The men were on his doorstep in minutes, and said, "Sir, we have instructions to take your telephone." The man softened, and said, "Fellas, I just got a little bit worked up and said some things I didn't mean. Why don't you let me call the lady back and apologize, and then you can take the phone." The repairmen agreed, and waited as the man dialed the phone company back. When the lady answered, the man asked apologetically, "Are you the woman that I told to take this phone and shove it?" "Yes," she replied coldly. Still speaking tenderly, the man said, "Well, I just wanted to call you and tell you [At this point, pause, then change your voice to a more upbeat tone as you say:] GET READY, THEY'RE BRINGING IT OVER!"

I don't know about you, but I don't think this guy helped his case very much. We all have a tendency to get bent out of shape when we're under stress, and to make things far worse than they were before.

EXAMPLE #37: THE LAWS OF DEFLATION AND PROMPTING

A truck driver was being given his annual test to renew his license. His examiner asked him: "Jimmy, suppose you were coming down a mountain in your eighteen-wheeler, and the brakes went out. What would you do?" Jimmy thought for a moment and said, "I would apply my emergency brake." The examiner said: "Good. But suppose you were coming down that mountain and your emergency brake failed, too. Then what would you do?" Jimmy said, "Well, I'd turn on my hazard lights, and honk my horn to warn other vehicles, and look for an emergency truck turnout." The examiner said, "Good again. But suppose you were coming down a mountain, both of your brakes failed, and none of your lights or your horn worked, and when you looked ahead of you there was a truck ahead of you in your lane, and another one in the other lane headed your way, and there was no room to pull off on either side of the road?" Jimmy said quickly: "I'd wake up Johnny." The examiner was baffled. "Who's Johnny?" he asked. Jimmy said, "Well, Johnny's my partner. He sleeps behind me when I'm driving, and I sleep when he's driving." "Okay," said the examiner, "Why would you wake up Johnny?" Jimmy said, "Well, it's like this. Johnny's from a small town. [At this point, change your facial expression from one of deep thought to one of surprise as you say:] AND HE AIN'T NEVER SEEN NUTHIN' LIKE WHAT'S ABOUT TO HAPPEN!"

That's how I feel when I look at the potential of this company. We ain't never seen nuthin' like what's about to happen!

EXAMPLE #38: THE LAWS OF DEFLATION AND PROMPTING

This story is about a salesman who used his stuttering problem to his advantage. Even though common sense tells us that the punch line would naturally be characterized by the same stuttering as the rest of the salesman's words, the law of deflation demands that it be told smoothly and quickly. Otherwise, the story is emptied of its humor. In fact, unless told suddenly, it evokes sympathy for the stutterer and disappointment in the storyteller rather than the laughter intended.

A man with a stuttering problem somehow made his living selling Bibles door to door. In fact, he was the leading Bible salesman in his company. One day, the sales manager called a meeting and asked him to share the secrets of his effectiveness with the other sales people, which he did. He stood up and said: "I kn-n-n-ock on the d-d-d-d-oor. A-a-a-a-nd when the l-l-l-l-ady of the h-h-h-h-ouse answers, I say: 'H-h-h-h-ello, my name is B-b-b-b-ill and I s-s-s-s-sell B-b-b-b-b-ibles. W-w-w-w-would you like to b-b-b-b-buy one, or w-w-w-w-w-WOULD YOU LIKE ME TO READ IT TO YOU?'"

You know, no matter what your particular problem or handicap, I'm convinced that there's a way to turn it to your advantage, if you just think creatively enough.

EXAMPLE #39: THE LAWS OF DEFLATION AND PROMPTING

In this next story, note that once the word "iceberg" is stated, the audience has all of the pieces necessary to fully understand the joke. Consequently, the words that follow it, "You're all alike", must be said immediately afterwards, with almost no pause. However, because the punch line is a play off of the Chinese man's similar statement, there must be some pause in order to mirror it properly. The solution is to make it a very *brief* pause.

A Jewish man and a Chinese man happened into the same pub at about the same time and sat at opposite ends of the bar. As the night wore on, each of them got a little bit drunk, and the Jewish man began to scowl at the Chinese man. Eventually, he sauntered down to the end of the bar, and belted the Chinese fellow right in the mouth. The guy fell off his stool, landed on his back, and said, "What did you do that for?!?" The Jewish man replied, "That was for Pearl Harbor!" The Chinese man couldn't believe his ears. He said, "You idiot, that was the Japanese; I'm Chinese!" Returning to his stool, the Jewish man snorted, "Japanese, Chinese, Korean, you're all alike." Well, before long, the Chinese man wandered down to the end of the bar and belted the Jewish man in the mouth, triumphantly shouting, "That was for the Titanic!" The Jewish man said, "What in the world are you talking about?" The Chinese man stuck his nose in the air and as he walked off said, "Greenberg, Goldberg, Iceberg, [pause briefly] YOU'RE ALL ALIKE!"

Isn't it funny how we can take one look at a person, size them up, and blame all of the world's ills on them because of their nationality, or the color of their skin, or the style of their clothing?

EXAMPLE #40: THE LAWS OF DEFLATION AND PROMPTING

A clever story about a referee and an angry football player employs all of the laws discussed thus far. It inflates very nicely by virtue of each character's evaluation of the events that took place in the train car. And it deflates quickly with an unexpected ending. Notice that the first half of the punch line is extraneous, but reveals enough information to enable an astute person to figure out the remainder quickly. Therefore, it is essential that the heart of the punch line be delivered immediately after first half of the sentence, thus allowing the audience no time to think of the outcome on their own. Furthermore, the punch line reveals that the football player slaps the official. By mimicking the slapping motion as you tell the story (if you do so in an upward direction, not downward), you can naturally cue the audience to laugh by virtue of your already upturned palm. As always, the punch line must be delivered with abandon.

The story goes that a football player was penalized for holding on what would have been the game's winning play for his team that day. The touchdown was nullified, his team lost, and he was the goat of the game. He was furious with the official who made the call, and by coincidence ended up in the same train compartment with that referee for the trip home. Also in the same compartment was a woman and her beautiful 20 year old daughter. At one point, the train entered a tunnel, and the compartment was plunged into darkness. There, in the darkened compartment, all four heard two distinct sounds. The first was a kiss, and the second was a slap. As they emerged into the light again, the mother had a very proud expression on her face. She figured that in the darkness, the football player had tried to steal a kiss from her daughter, but she had been proper enough to slap him for it. The daughter was amazed that a mature man like this official had been so brazen as to kiss her mother in the darkened car, but more than a little satisfied that her mom had slapped him for the attempt. The official was little upset. He figured that the football player had tried to kiss the young girl, who had tried to slap him, but in the darkness had missed and hit the referee. In fact, the only one in the compartment who knew what had really happened was the football player, for under cover of darkness, he had loudly kissed the back of his own hand, AND THEN SLAPPED THE FOOL OUT OF THE REFEREE!

I love creativity, don't you? It's that ability to look at a problem and come up with a solution that no one else would have thought of.

LAW FIVE

The Law of Exaggeration

The tension and anticipation necessary to produce big laughs can be greatly enhanced by several factors, the first of which is the use of hyperbole. Employing exaggeration can cause people to smile, maybe to chuckle, and to look forward to the punch line with greater anticipation. Consequently, instead of saying a "big" guy walked into the saloon, it is better to say that a "gargantuan man walked in, with his knuckles dragging the floor." You might even add that he was "about three hundred feet tall," or some such nonsense. The yarns in this section all include this helpful device.

EXAMPLE #41: THE LAW OF EXAGGERATION

Note in the following story that the exaggeration being used is not in any way germane to the point of the joke. The punch line, itself, would be just as funny if the young lawyer had pretended to talk with any unnamed client. However, having him speak in such familiar terms with the Rockefellers makes the joke as a whole funnier, because of the added tension the hyperbole creates within the listener.

A young man graduated from law school and was just moving into his new office. He was setting up his files in preparation for his new practice, when he heard the elevator open and footsteps coming down the hall toward his office. Not wanting the potential client to know that he had never tried a case before, he quickly grabbed the telephone and pretended to be handling an important case. The visitor stood in the doorway waiting for him to finish. "Yes sir, Mr. Rockefeller," the lawyer said, "we have your case fully under control and we'll be ready for the trial tomorrow at noon. Tell Mrs. Rockefeller Tuesday night is fine for dinner. Oysters are a great choice. Yeah. Bye Bye." He looked up as though he was too busy to be interrupted, and said, *"Yes, can I help you?" "I'm not sure,"* came the reply. *"I'M FROM THE PHONE COMPANY AND I'M HERE TO HOOK UP YOUR PHONE!"*

Pretending to be something you're not rarely works, does it?

EXAMPLE #42: THE LAW OF EXAGGERATION

In the following example, two exaggerations are used. One concerns the poverty level of the two cowboys who are the joke's principal characters. Instead of merely telling your audience that they were looking for a few extra bucks, you can increase the humor of the joke by saying they didn't have two nickels to rub together. You could even interject a "they were *so* poor joke," if you wish. Secondly, the two cowboys end up surrounded by Indians. The story would be funny if they were surrounded by fifty Indians. It becomes hilarious just by exaggerating the number to the point where they were surrounded by Indians in every direction as far as the eye could see, all on horseback, wearing war paint, and brandishing spears.

Indians raided a town in the Old West, scalping dozens of frontiersmen. The remaining townsfolk were so angry that they offered a reward of fifty dollars for every Indian scalp that might be brought in. Well, a couple of cowpokes who didn't have two nickels to rub together decided to go out in search of Indian scalps. That night they slept by their campfire, and when the first one awoke in the morning, he could see that they were surrounded by Indians as far as the eye could see in every direction, all on horseback, wearing war paint and brandishing spears. The guy shook his friend excitedly. He said: "Tex! Tex! Wake up! WE'RE ABOUT TO BECOME MILLIONAIRES!"

I love an optimist, don't you? But sometimes optimism isn't necessarily called for.

EXAMPLE #43: THE LAW OF EXAGGERATION

Sometimes, the use of exaggeration is the key ingredient to making a story funny. For instance, in this next example, the story is humorous in direct proportion to the amount of money wagered by the principal character. A bet of four dollars would make the story pointless. A bet of $444,444 makes it hysterical.

There was once a superstitious man who took a business trip to Miami. He left on April 4, 1994. (That's 4/4/94.) His flight number was, coincidentally, 444. When he arrived, he noted that his secretary had made his reservations at the Four Seasons Hotel, and his room number was 4444. At precisely 4:00 p.m., a colleague called him and said, "Let's go down to the dog track and do some betting." They took the bus. (It was bus number 44.) And it arrived at the dog track at exactly 4:44 p.m. Well, the man saw a pattern. He quickly scanned the list of dogs, and sure enough, in the fourth race, dog number 4 was named "Four Roses." He went to the betting window, and took out his American Express Card, and bet $444,444 dollars on that horse. And wouldn't you know it? HE CAME IN FOURTH!

Sometimes there seems to be a pattern to our world, like there really is a God orchestrating life. Other times there seems to be no rhyme or reason to anything.

EXAMPLE #44: THE LAW OF EXAGGERATION

The following joke capitalizes on a ridiculously cheap cruise and an absurd scenario. The story is made funnier by the exaggerations it contains than by the punch line, itself. For example, if the cruise were reduced to only $175.00 instead of $20, and if the cruise ship were a rowboat instead of an inner tube, and if the participants were wearing swimsuits instead of their underwear, the humor of it would be reduced. Note that the substance of the joke would remain unchanged, yet its overall effect on the audience would be greatly diminished.

The story goes that a young man was driving to the beach one day for vacation, contemplating how he would spend his week off. He saw a billboard by the road that said: "Take a cruise, only $20." He thought this sounded like just what the doctor ordered, so he pulled into the place and said, "I'd like to take your cruise." The travel agent said, "You do understand, of course, that this is the economy cruise." "No problem," said the motorist as he placed twenty dollars on the counter. So they took him in the back, stripped him down to his underwear, handed him an inner tube and threw him in the ocean. He floated around for several hours, and eventually washed up on a deserted island, where he stopped to rest. By sheer coincidence, another young man was driving down that same highway that day, saw the same billboard advertising a cruise for only twenty dollars, and pulled in to

44

check it out. The travel agent said, "You do realize that this is the economy cruise, don't you?" "No problem," the man said, and placed two sawbucks on the counter. They took him in the back, stripped him down to his underwear, handed him an inner tube, and threw him in the ocean. By sheer coincidence, he eventually washed up on the same deserted island and stopped to rest on the same beach where the first traveler was still sitting. After a few minutes, the second guy said to the first one, "Do you suppose they serve dinner on this cruise?" The first one thought for a moment and said, "I'm not sure, BUT THEY DIDN'T LAST YEAR!"

Now this guy had a problem. He made the same mistakes over and over again. And I think that we may be guilty of the same thing.

EXAMPLE #45: THE LAW OF EXAGGERATION

This hilarious story is enhanced by the number of ants being killed as it progresses. The greater the exaggeration of the size of the anthill, and the number of ants killed, and the adjectives used to describe the killing (i.e. slaughter, massacre, etc.) the funnier the joke will be. Note that it also features not only a poor golfer, but the "world's worst" golfer. All are exaggerations.

The world's worst golfer was out on the course one afternoon, and sliced a tee shot way off into the woods. He finally found it on top of the largest ant hill he had ever seen. Not wanting to take a penalty stroke, he decided to play it from there. He took a swing and completely missed the ball, killing about forty thousand ants in the process. He swung again, digging deeper into the ant hill, killing another sixty thousand ants. Twenty swings later, he had still not touched the ball, but had produced the worst ant massacre in history. Millions of dying ants lay all over the ground. Amid all this confusion, two ants crawled up out of their hole and observed this catastrophe unfolding for a few seconds. Then one of them turned to the other and said, "You know, if we don't get on the ball, WE'RE GONNA DIE!"

I'm convinced that just like the ants, if we don't get on the ball, this business is gonna die.

LAW SIX

The Law of Personality

Further anticipation can be created in the telling of a story by giving stereotyped personalities or names to the characters in it. For example, a Texan might be referred to as Tex (as was used in Example #42) and drive a car that's 300 feet long. In a story included later in this book, a Texas oil millionaire is said to have a daughter. Simply stating this fact would be sufficient, but this does nothing to build the tension necessary to produce uncontrollable laughter in an audience. So, whenever I tell this particular story, I have the oil man describe her as "my lovely daughter, Bonnie Lou." Note that naming her "Susan" or "Mary" would not help, because the name must be consistent with a humorous stereotype of the sort of person being described. Further examples might be a nerd named Eugene, or a hooker named Roxanne, or a gangster named Bugsy.

EXAMPLE #46: THE LAW OF PERSONALITY

I heard the following story used by author and speaker Zig Ziglar several years ago. It features a high and mighty professor whom I have named Dr. Snootwick, adding to the humor of the story.

A Psychology professor by the name of Dr. Snootwick had no children of his own, yet was still very vocal about his theories on child rearing. Whenever he saw a neighbor scolding or spanking a child for some wrongdoing, the professor would sanctimoniously say, "You should love your child, not punish him." One hot summer afternoon the professor was laying a new sidewalk in front of his house. Exhausted after hours of labor, he laid down his trowel, wiped the perspi-

ration from his forehead, and walked toward the house. Suddenly out of the corner of his eye he saw a neighborhood boy dart through the yard and jump with both feet into the wet cement. The professor was incensed. He ran over, picked up the boy and began to spank him furiously. Just then a neighbor mocked him from a nearby yard: "Hey Dr. Snootwick, don't you remember that you're supposed to love that child, not punish him?" The professor shouted back furiously: "I do love him in the abstract, BUT NOT IN THE CONCRETE!"

It's easy to love people in the abstract, isn't it? But genuine love goes beyond the abstract to concrete expressions of compassion even when it is not deserved.

EXAMPLE #47: THE LAW OF PERSONALITY

In the following story, the woman is given the name Maude to enhance her status as the loyal, reliable housewife.

There was once an elderly couple sitting on a porch swing reminiscing about their lives together. The man leaned over to his wife, touched her hand, and said, "You know, Maude, I was just thinking about how you've always been there for me. Do you remember right after we met in college, how I lost my job and you had to go to work to help pay my tuition?" Maude nodded silently. "You were there for me," the man continued. "And do you remember how we almost got on our feet that time, but I fell asleep smoking a cigarette, and burned the house down? If it weren't for your inheritance, we couldn't have gotten by." Maude nodded again. "You were there," he said. "And do you remember how I lost our life savings a few years ago in that all night poker game? You didn't get mad, you just pawned your engagement ring to get us by." Again, Maude nodded. "You were there," he said, now shedding a few quiet tears. "And do you remember how last year the bank foreclosed on our house and we had to move in here with the kids? You were there for me." Finally, Maude spoke up. She said, "Yes, we've been through all of that together." As if having a new revelation, the man turned to his wife, wiped away his tears, and said, "You know, Maude... YOU'RE A JINX!"

Isn't it amazing how all of us can find a way to blame somebody else for our problems? And yet, the key to solving our problems is learning to take responsibility for them ourselves.

EXAMPLE #48: THE LAW OF PERSONALITY

Giving names to the mischievous little boys in the next two stories adds personality and, therefore, tension to them.

Around the turn of the century there was little boy named Jimmy who liked to accompany his mom to the local country store. In that store there was huge barrel of molasses, which was dipped out and sold in whatever amount the customers wanted. Jimmy got into the habit of dipping his finger in the molasses and licking it, which greatly irritated the store owner. One day, after catching the boy licking up the molasses again, the owner in desperation decided to teach the boy a lesson. He picked him up and dropped him into the barrel. And as Jimmy's head disappeared beneath the surface, he could be heard saying this prayer: "Oh Lord, MAKE MY TONGUE EQUAL TO THIS OPPORTUNITY."

As I stand before you today, that's my prayer as well.

EXAMPLE #49: THE LAW OF PERSONALITY

Johnny and Bobby were the terrors of the fourth grade, and were frequently sent to the school principal for correction. One day the principal, tired of this almost daily ritual, decided that what the two boys needed was not a lecture, but a good dose of religion. But being in a public school, he knew that he would have to be careful about what he said. Instead of waiting for the boys to be dispatched to his office as usual, he decided to be pro-active, and sent for them. They arrived, and the principal summoned Johnny first, leaving the puzzled Bobby to wait in the lobby. The principal sat down with the first boy and said sternly, "Johnny, I have a question for you and I want you to think about it long and hard: Where is God? Where is God?" Johnny had no idea how to answer, so he sat silently. The principal said, "Johnny, I'm going to ask you one more time: Where is God?" Again, Johnny was silent. The principal, satisfied with himself, said: "Now Johnny you just think about that question. Now go wait in the lobby and send Bobby in here." Shaken, Johnny walked slowly to the lobby and told his friend to go speak with the principal. Bobby said, "I'll go talk to him, but before I do, tell me what all this is about." Johnny thought for a minute, and said, "I'm not sure exactly. BUT APPARENTLY GOD IS MISSING AND THEY'RE TRYING TO PIN IT ON US!"

You know, this principal suffered from a problem common to all of us: a breakdown in communication. And I think a huge percentage of the problems we face in our businesses, our marriages, and our churches can be traced to this root cause.

EXAMPLE #50: THE LAW OF PERSONALITY

Sometimes personality can be injected into characters by your mannerisms. In this joke, acting very stiff or nerdish as you deliver the lines from the mathematician and the statistician will make them come alive to your audience, as well as enhance the contrast between their response and that of the politician. The politician's line should be delivered slyly, as though he is cutting a deal under the table.

The story goes that three men were applying for the same job. One of them was a mathematician, another a statistician, and another a politician. In order to save time, the interviewer decided to limit the interview to a single question, and the man who gave the best answer would be hired. He asked the mathematician: "What is two plus two?" The man answered, "Two plus two is four point zero, zero, zero, repeating ad infinitum." He turned to the statistician and repeated the question. The man took out his calculator and figured for a while. Finally, he replied, "Two plus two equals one hundred percent of four, with a potential error margin of plus or minus 3%." The question was repeated for the politician, who then leaned forward, and replied: "WHAT DO YOU WANT IT TO BE?"

There seems to be a huge integrity crisis in government these days. The men and women we send to Washington seem to be telling everyone exactly what they want to hear, with no regard for the truth. But integrity is the cornerstone of any legitimate government.

EXAMPLE #51: THE LAW OF PERSONALITY

One final way to capitalize on the law of personality is to tell a joke on yourself or on a popular person in your audience. The following story is most effective when told about yourself, so it is written in the first person.

I used to own a huge sheep farm with several thousand sheep. My ram died, so I went out and spent $6000 on what they said was the finest ram on the east coast. But unfortunately, he just stayed in his pen. He wouldn't associate with any of the lady sheep. So I took him to the vet, and he told me to give him a particular *pill once a day for a month. Well, I started doing so and, sure enough, within two days he was out in the fields "socializing" with every sheep in the pack all day every day. They were funny little pills, about the size of a marble, bright red [pause]. In fact, THEY TASTE A LITTLE LIKE PEPPERMINT...!*

Wouldn't it be nice if there were a pill that could deal with all of the problems of life that easily?

LAW SEVEN

The Law of Inflection

Any time you can add an appropriate accent or dialect to the words spoken by the characters in your joke, you will add to the "tension" on your balloon, making the "pop" all the more explosive. For example, if the person in my story is an elderly woman, I deliver her lines by using the most ancient voice I can muster. Note that the dialect must be greatly exaggerated. Simply talking like a fifty-year-old woman will not help you. In fact, it might be perceived as an insult to middle-aged women - not a good way to get a laugh! However, talking like a *hundred* year old woman will. Similarly, in a joke about a Texan, I deliver his lines with an outrageous mockery of a Texas drawl. As a result, people are ready to burst out laughing before the punch line is ever delivered.

An exception to this rule, of course, would be those cases in which the use of a dialect or accent would be considered an ethnic slur. If this is the case, even the funniest joke will evoke only anger from some members of the audience, and should be avoided like toxic waste. A generally safe accent is an exaggerated Southern or Texas drawl. The next several stories involve ethnic or regional accents that are relatively safe for your use.

EXAMPLE #52: THE LAW OF INFLECTION

This delightful bit of witticism features a Mexican bandito, and the humor of it is significantly enhanced by the use of a Mexican accent when delivering his lines, and those of the interpreter.

In the old West there lived a crafty Mexican bandito by the name of George (pronounced hor-hay) Rodriguez. He would swim across the Rio Grande by night, rob a bank in one of the border towns of Texas, and be safely back in Mexico before anyone knew the robbery had taken place. This happened so frequently that one particular Texas Marshall became obsessed with apprehending him. So one morning, after Rodriguez had robbed a bank of more than a million dollars, the lawman was so incensed that he decided to pursue him across the border. He tracked him to a crowded saloon, walked up to him, and put a gun to his head. He growled: "Rodriguez, you had better tell me where the money is right now, or I'll blow your brains out." To his surprise, the terrified bandit began yelling: "Pero Senor, no hablo Ingles!" The Marshall hadn't counted on this. Sensing the lawman's dilemma, a wiry Mexican man stepped up and said: "I am the only one here who speaks English." The Marshall said, "Well tell this crook what I said." The man explained carefully that the Marshall wanted to know where the money was, or he would shoot him on the spot. The bandito replied in Spanish: "One mile north of town there is an old abandoned well. The money is in there. Just don't shoot!" The translator turned to the Marshall and said, "He says... HE'S READY TO DIE!"

They say that what you don't know can't hurt you. I beg to differ. The Texas Marshall didn't know Spanish, and it cost him the recovery of a million dollars. George Rodriguez didn't know English, and it cost him his life. As the translator knew, your most valuable asset in business is knowledge.

EXAMPLE #53: THE LAW OF INFLECTION

Using a Jewish accent on the punch line of this joke will greatly increase its humor.

A tourist took a trip to the Holy Land, and went to the temple mount in Jerusalem. Of course, the temple has long since been destroyed, and all that remains is a part of the retaining wall on the side of the mountain. We know it as the wailing wall. Hundreds of thousands of Orthodox Jews have made it their practice to go there to pray. They stand facing the wall, sometimes touching the wall, as they pray. The tourist watched these men praying for a few minutes, and decided he would strike up a conversation with one of them. He walked up to one man who had finished praying, and was turning to leave. He said, "Tell me, sir, does God ever answer your prayers when you come to pray here?" The man *slowly shook his head, sighed, and said, "SOMETIMES IT'S LIKE TALKING TO A WALL!"*

Have you ever felt that way when you talk to God?

EXAMPLE #54: THE LAW OF INFLECTION

The punch line of the following story is best told without emotion in the staccato, stereotypical American Indian accent.

A lady was walking down the street one day, when she saw an Indian lying in the road with his ear to the ground. As she approached him, she heard him saying: "Lincoln Town car, black with burgundy interior, mag wheels, headed west...." The woman was amazed. She said, "Sir, do you mean you can tell all that from just listening to the ground?" The Indian said, "No. THAT CAR JUST RAN OVER ME."

I'll bet that there are a lot of people that work for this company that at the end of a typical work day can be found lying in their office floor mumbling: "Three irate customers, headed west."

EXAMPLE #55: THE LAW OF INFLECTION

The next two stories employ oriental accents.

Three soldiers were living together during the Korean war, and were waited on by a Korean house-boy who cooked and cleaned for them. This house-boy was the model of politeness. Whatever he was told to do, he did it instantly and without complaint. But whenever he made the slightest mistake, the soldiers would explode with rage. The house-boy never reacted. So the soldiers responded by playing practical jokes on the boy. They would short-sheet his bed, nail his shoes to the floor, etc. Well, eventually the soldiers began to feel guilty about the way they were treating the boy, and went to him to apologize. The boy listened and said, "So, you no more yell at me?" "No," they said, "We won't yell at you any more." "No more short-sheet bed?" he inquired. "No, no more short-sheet bed." "No more nail shoes to floor?" "No, we promise we'll never nail your shoes to the floor again." Satisfied, the young Korean nodded and said, "Good. Then... NO MORE SPIT IN SOUP."

Different people show their anger in different ways. But regardless, anger can be dangerous.

EXAMPLE #56: THE LAW OF INFLECTION

This story is one of the few in which two different accents are helpful. Generally the use of two accents clutters the joke and actually detracts from its humor. However, I believe that using an Oriental accent for the two Japanese boys, and an exaggerated southern accent for the other student's will increase it's humor. If one of the accents is to be omitted, it should be the oriental accent, because it is more important to use the accent on the punch line.

A not-too-bright student was asked to stand before his history class one day to answer a question. "Who said, 'Give me liberty or give me death'?" the teacher asked. The student shrugged and said, "I don't know." There were two Japanese transfer students in the front row - twin brothers - who both raised their hands and shouted, "I know, I know! It was Patrick Henry!" The teacher commended them, and asked the first student another question: "Who said, 'I regret that I have but one life to give for my country'?" Again, the student was baffled. But the two Japanese students shouted, "I know! It was Nathan Hale!" "Right again," said the teacher. She dismissed the first student, who went to his desk, leaned over to a friend, and said, "I'm going to whip the fool out of those little Japs!" The teacher spun around and said, "Who said that?" The student jumped up and said, "DOUGLAS MACARTHUR!"

It does seem that other nations are starting to out-produce the United States in areas like education, doesn't it?

EXAMPLE #57: THE LAW OF INFLECTION

Some of the funniest jokes are those in which the punch line is actually spoken by God. I've found that I can add to the humor of such stories by cupping my hands around a microphone, putting my mouth right up against it, and speaking in a slow, deep voice. The result is a booming God-like effect, which is quite funny. These next two jokes benefit significantly from such treatment.

A Methodist preacher and a Baptist preacher called in sick to their respective churches one Sunday and went to the golf course. The Baptist preacher was a terrible golfer, and on the first tee, he swung with all of his might and missed the ball completely. He lost his temper and shouted, "Darn, I hate it when I miss!"

54

Just then the two preachers heard a booming voice from above saying: "Lightning bolts were meant for people who say that word!" The Baptist preacher took another swing, completely missing the ball. Again, he shouted, "Darn, I hate it when I miss!" The booming voice was heard again: "I said lightning bolts were made for people who use that word!" The Baptist preacher swung and missed again, following the miss with yet another, "Darn, I hate when I miss!" The booming voice was angry this time: "I told you that lightning bolts were made for people who say that word!" Just then the sky lit up with an incredibly brilliant flash of lightning, and the air was filled with an overpowering thunderclap. But when the smoke cleared, there lay the Methodist preacher burnt to a cinder! The puzzled Baptist preacher then heard the voice from heaven again. This time it said, "DARN, I HATE IT WHEN I MISS!"'

Don't you hate when you miss? Isn't it amazing that one miss in the investment game, or the commodities business, or the [fill in your own field] business can leave you burnt to a cinder? How can we limit or eliminate those costly misses?

EXAMPLE #58: THE LAW OF INFLECTION

A guy decided to try his hand at ice fishing. So he took his fishing gear and walked out onto the ice. He had just begun to chisel a hole in the ice, when he heard a booming voice from above. It said: "There are no fish under there." The man shrugged his shoulders, picked up his gear and moved about fifty feet away, where he began chiseling a new hole. Again, the booming voice thundered, "There are no fish under there." And once again, the man moved to a new spot and began to cut a hole. This time, the voice was more insistent: "I said there are no fish under there!" The man stopped chiseling, looked up and shouted, "Are you God?" The voice thundered back, "No. I'M THE RINK MANAGER!"

How can you tell the voice of God from the voice of mere human beings? How can you be sure that when you make a decision it's in harmony with what God wants for your life?

EXAMPLE #59: THE LAW OF INFLECTION

The next four examples feature central characters who are elderly (or appear elderly, in one case). For maximum effect, their voices throughout each story should be delivered in the voice of an ancient (not merely elderly) person.

*An elderly couple was sitting on the front porch swing on a beautiful
evening. "Oh, Fred," she said softly, "Do you remember how you used to hold my
hand?" Fred reached out and tenderly took her hand. After a while she said,
"Fred, do you remember how you used to put your arm around me?" Fred snug-
gled up close and gently put his arm around her. A while later she said, "Fred, do
you remember how you used to nibble on my ear?" With that, Fred jumped up
and went in the house. She was completely taken aback, and shouted, "Darling,
did I say something to offend you?" Fred shouted back: "Nope. JUST GOIN' IN
TO GET MY TEETH!"*

I don't guess it would be too pleasant to a woman to have her ears
gummed. No, you need teeth for some jobs, and I'm here to help give your
sales force some teeth.

EXAMPLE #60: THE LAW OF INFLECTION

*An elderly man and woman were seated in rocking chairs on their front porch
one day. It was their seventieth wedding anniversary, and the old man wanted to
say something nice to his wife. He said, "Honey, I'm proud of you." Being very
hard of hearing, she said, "What'd you say?" He repeated himself: "Honey, I'm
proud of you." She cupped her hand to her ear and responded: "Ehhhh?" The
man shouted as best he could: "I said I'm proud of you!" The woman gave an
understanding nod, settled back into her rocker and said, "Yeah. I'M TIRED OF
YOU, TOO."*

One of the biggest obstacles to any relationship is communication.

EXAMPLE #61: THE LAW OF INFLECTION

*A elderly man was terribly afraid of flying, and had refused all his life to
ever get on an airplane. But, his family finally coaxed him aboard one. He sat
tensely throughout the flight, his knuckles white on the arm rests. When the
plane landed, the family gathered around him and said, "Now that wasn't so
bad, was it, Pop?" He replied, "Well, I still don't trust them things. Why, the
whole time we were in the air, NOT ONCE DID I EVER PUT MY FULL WEIGHT
DOWN!"*

You know, a lot of people treat God that way, too. They trust Him a little
bit, but not completely. They're willing to ride with God, but they can never
quite bring themselves to put down their full weight of trust.

EXAMPLE #62: THE LAW OF INFLECTION

There was once a young man who was contemplating the meaning of life. He recalled having seen a very old man in a rocking chair on a front porch across town, and decided to pay him a visit. He found the old man in his rocker and said, "Wise old man, what is the meaning of life?" The man stroked his beard and said, "The meaning of life is... party hearty, go for all the gusto, light up the night, after all you only go around once in life." The young man pondered these words and said, "Wise old man, that's a very interesting philosophy, but how does it affect your daily life?" The old man said, "Well, I drink three six packs of beer every day, I smoke two packs of cigarettes a day, I dance every night until three a.m., and I never take a bath." The young man said, "Sir, that's remarkable. Just how old are you?" The man replied "TWENTY-TWO."

The moral of the story is that not everyone in this world who appears wise *is* wise. Sometimes they are fools. And similarly, not all of the people in this world who appear to be fools are necessarily foolish. And telling the difference between the two is one of life's most formidable tasks.

EXAMPLE #63: THE LAW OF INFLECTION

When a joke contains lines by a preacher, it is often beneficial to deliver his sermon lines in a syrupy-sweet, sing-song type of voice. That will help greatly in the following story, but should be avoided in the punch line. This is because the sing-song style is too slow for a punch line, and will actually detract from the humor of the joke.

A young preacher was becoming discouraged with the ministry because he couldn't get people to pay attention to his sermons. Each week his audience slowly drifted off to sleep. He asked an older minister what to do. The old man said, "Son, you have to start with a statement that is startling and shocking. That will get their attention and keep them awake." "But what can I say that will startle them?" the young preacher asked. The old man said, "This Sunday is Mother's Day. When you step into the pulpit to preach, open by saying: 'Some of the happiest hours of my life were spent in the arms of another man's wife.' Pause to let it sink in, then repeat yourself. Then, pause again. Finally, when you have them right on the edges of their seats, say: 'Of course, I am referring to the arms of my dear mother.'" The young minister decided to give it a try. He strode confidently to the pulpit and began by saying: "Some of the happiest hours of my life were spent in the arms of another man's wife." Now the

57

preacher had made one huge mistake. He had forgotten to tell his wife about the story. No sooner had he gotten these words out of his mouth than her face began to turn red; she set her jaw and began to steam. And when he repeated himself, she could not contain herself. She heaved her hymnal at him, nailing him between the eyes. Then she began climbing over pews to get to him. She grabbed him around the throat and began choking him. Eventually the minister was able to dislodge her hands long enough to assure her that it was not as she thought, and if she would just let him finish the story, everything would be all right. Well, she stepped back to let him continue. By now, though, the young preacher was so flustered that he had lost his place in his notes. He said, "Some of the happiest hours of my life were spent in the arms of another man's wife...." He fumbled through his notes, hunting for the punch line. He stammered, "Some of the happiest hours of my life were spent in the arms of another man's wife...." Realizing he was not going to find his place in his notes, he finally blurted out: "BUT FOR THE LIFE OF ME I CAN'T REMEMBER WHO SHE WAS!"

It's funny how we all react under pressure, isn't it?

EXAMPLE #64: THE LAW OF INFLECTION

One of the funniest accents that can be used is the aforementioned southern drawl. In order to avoid offending people, the accent must be greatly exaggerated, with the result that no one in your audience actually talks that way. Try using such an accent as you deliver the punch line of this cute anecdote.

An elderly man got tired of fighting the cold weather up north, and was advised by his doctor to retire to Florida. The first day he was there, he went to the beach. But looking at all the lovely ladies over-stressed his heart to the point that he died. They carted his body to the undertaker, who did a masterful job of embalming him, making him look twenty years younger. Then they shipped his body back home to New York, and at the wake two elderly ladies stopped by the casket to pay their respects. After seeing him all decked out in the coffin, one of them turned to the other and said, "You know, Eunice, I THINK THAT TRIP TO FLORIDA DONE HIM GOOD."

A lot of churches specialize in dressing up spiritually dead people to make them look good. What they really need to do is bring people to life, regardless of how they might appear outwardly.

OR...

I wonder how much time in this company is spent dressing up dead products or programs instead of creating new ones that are fresh and alive.

EXAMPLE #65: THE LAW OF INFLECTION

The following example is one in which the punch line is delivered by a small child. If you can imitate a little girl's voice well, doing so will help you create laughter with this charming story. However, if you cannot imitate a little girl with great accuracy, do not attempt to do so at all. The joke will work almost as well with no change in inflection at all. If you omit the child's inflection, you can use the voice of a sweet southern housewife when you speak the lines of the neighbor lady. Be prepared for the fact that the laughs from this joke are usually delayed, but gradually grow from a chuckle to outright hilarity as the full implications of the punch line sink in. So give it a little extra time.

The story goes that a four-year old girl and a two-year old boy decided to play house. She played the wife, and he played the husband. As husband and wife, they paid a visit to the neighbor lady who said, "Well, hello. What can I do for you today?" The little girl politely said, "Good afternoon. We are playing house. This is my husband, and I am his wife, and we decided to drop by for some lemonade and cookies." The lady was delighted. She said, "Do come in." She served them some cookies and lemonade. The lady and the little girl chatted politely while the little boy sat quietly. After a few minutes, the lady said, "Would you like some more lemonade and cookies?" The little girl replied, "No thank you. We must go now, because MY HUSBAND HAS JUST WET HIS PANTS."

I think that story is a very telling commentary on the state of our society: the female doing all she can to live up to the responsibilities of being an adult, while the male is making all of the same messes he was making as a little boy.

EXAMPLE #66: THE LAW OF INFLECTION

An important exception to the law of inflection is this: it does not apply to lines that are attributed to an animal. For example, the next story contains a punch line delivered by a parrot. In all talking animal jokes, the animal's lines should be delivered in your normal voice. Trying to imitate the parrot (or dog, or cat, etc.) will confuse your audience; they will not know whether to laugh at your idea of what an animal sounds like or at the punch line, and instead of laughing at either, they will try to figure it out. By the time they answer their own question, it will be too late to laugh at all. The tension has dissipated. The balloon has fizzled, and can no longer be popped.

The story goes that a Catholic Priest got a little bit lonely one day, so he went down to a pet store, and purchased a parrot named George. Over the next few months, this priest painstakingly trained this parrot to do what no other bird had done before - he taught that bird to pray. The priest even put a string of rosary beads in the cage and taught the parrot how to use them. Well, as you can imagine, the priest was so happy with the results that he decided to teach another bird how to pray. So he went back to the pet store and this time he purchased a female parrot. He placed her in the cage with George. And no sooner had the priest shut the cage door than George grabbed the rosary beads, slung them out of the cage and screamed, "PRAISE GOD, MY PRAYERS ARE ANSWERED!"

Now, the moral of the story is that God created males with a built-in affinity for females, and he designed females with an intrinsic attraction to males. The genders are distinct, not identical, as some would have us believe.

EXAMPLE #67: THE LAW OF INFLECTION

This next story features a talking lion. As in all animal voices, his lines should be delivered in your normal voice.

A violinist noticed that his music had a hypnotic effect on his audiences. Even dogs and cats would sit mesmerized as he played. He wondered if his playing would have the same effect on wild beasts, so he flew to Africa, went out into a jungle clearing and began to play. A lion, and elephant, and a gorilla charged out of the forest toward him, stopped to listen, and then sat down as though in a trance. Before long, the clearing was filled with all kinds of ferocious beasts, sitting spellbound as the man played. Suddenly, out of the brush came another lion who charged out of the jungle, pounced on the violinist, and killed him instantly. The first lion, said to him, "You idiot! Why did you do that?" The second lion said [cup a hand to your ear], "WHAT?

I hope you'll listen carefully to what I have to say here today, because if you don't hear me clearly you might try to kill me when I'm finished.

EXAMPLE #68: THE LAW OF INFLECTION

Another circumstance which necessitates a violation of the law of inflection is when using an accent would cause the emphasis of the story to be diverted from the main character. In the following story, an elderly man plays a minor role which is not critical to the outcome of the joke. His lines, if they cannot be omitted or merely described, should be delivered in your normal voice. To do otherwise will cause the story to lose focus.

A Catholic nun was driving down the highway one day when she ran out of gas. She walked back about a mile to a gas station she had seen by the road, and found that it was operated by a very old man. She told him of her predicament, and he replied, "Sister, I'd like to help you, but I don't have anything to put any gas in, and I'm too old to walk back to your car with you anyway." She prevailed upon him, and finally he rooted around and found the only thing in the station that would hold gasoline: his bedpan. He filled it up for her and gave her a funnel, and she walked back to her car. Now picture the scene. Here's a nun in her black and white habit pouring the contents of a bedpan into her tank. About that time a Cadillac comes zipping by at 70 m.p.h., screeches to a halt, and backs up to where the nun is still pouring the contents of this bedpan into her tank. A man sticks his head out the window, stares in unbelief, and after a couple of minutes says, "Sister, I WISH I HAD YOUR FAITH!"

Now, I submit to you that even if that bedpan had contained what the man thought it did, what that nun was exercising would still not have been faith. It would have been stupidity. And there's a whole lot of stupidity in this world masquerading as faith....

OR

I'll bet that there are people in this room right now who have quietly observed the lives of a few special people here, and thought, I wish I had their faith.

LAW EIGHT

The Law of Caricature

Often a joke will center around a negative emotion, such as fear, anger, or shock. This creates a dilemma for the comedian, because in the real world these emotions are anything but humorous. Delivering an "angry" line with an angry expression on your face, is therefore counter-productive. On the other hand, delivering it with no facial expression at all lessens the humor of the story. The solution to this sticky conundrum is to deliver such lines with the *caricature* of an angry or terrified person's facial expressions and voice. For example, the type of face Bugs Bunny makes when he's angry at Yosemite Sam is obviously an expression of anger, but it's humorous, not frightening. This is accomplished for the public speaker by greatly exaggerating your facial expressions and vocal inflections to cartoonish proportions.

Virtually any negative emotion can be caricatured in this way, as will be demonstrated in the following examples.

EXAMPLE #69: THE LAW OF CARICATURE

The emotion being highlighted in the next two stories is one of disgust or contempt. Remember that the punch lines must be delivered with a caricature of disgust, not with the genuine item.

A Baptist preacher wondered why offerings had been so low in his church, while the Catholic church down the street always had money to spare. So he decided to have a talk with the priest. "Father," he said, "how do you raise so much money?" The priest looked around to be sure no one was within earshot

62

and whispered: "I make it at the racetrack." The preacher couldn't believe his
ears, but went to the track to observe. He watched the priest go down to the
stable, walk up to a particular horse, and whisper in the animal's ear. Then the
priest bet his Sunday morning offering on that horse and won. This happened
for three straight races. The preacher excitedly ran to the bank and emptied his
church's bank account. He followed the priest down to the stable and watched
him cross himself and whisper in a horse's ear. The preacher then bet all his
church's money on that horse, and sat down to watch. His horse bolted from the
gate ahead of the others, and then began to extend his lead. The preacher was
ecstatic. Then suddenly, just before reaching the finish line, the horse stopped,
had a heart attack, and fell over dead. The preacher couldn't believe it. He found
the priest and screamed, "What's going on here? For three straight races you
whisper a blessing to a horse and he wins. But this time, you whisper in a horse's
ear, I bet all of my church's money on him, and he dies!" The priest shook his
head with disgust. He said, "You Baptists are so dumb. YOU DON'T EVEN KNOW
THE DIFFERENCE BETWEEN A BLESSING AND LAST RITES!"

**One of the keys to effective management, is determining when to put
your blessing on a particular project , and when to pronounce last rites on it.**

EXAMPLE #70: THE LAW OF CARICATURE

The story goes that a man decided to become a Trappist monk, so he headed
for the strictest monastery he could find. In fact, this particular order required a
vow of silence that limited him to speak only two words every ten years. He lived
in the monastery and, true to his vow, was silent for a decade. At the end of that
time, he was summoned before the leaders of the monastery to hear in two words
his assessment of the situation. They said, "Brother, what would you like to tell
us?" He thought for a moment and replied: "Food bad." They thanked him and
sent him away for ten more years, after which he appeared again before the com-
mittee. They said, "Brother, what do you have to tell us?" He inhaled and said,
"Bed hard." They sent him back to his room, and ten years later summoned him
again. They said, "Brother, what would you like to share with us?" The monk
sighed and said, "I quit." The members of the committee all shook their heads
and said with disgust, "We're not a bit surprised. Why, EVER SINCE YOU GOT
HERE YOU'VE DONE NOTHING BUT COMPLAIN!"

**Well, that seems like a harsh assessment for a guy who's only said six
words in thirty years, but the point is well-taken. People who complain all the
time aren't welcome anywhere.**

It should be noted that in telling the previous story, the punch line cannot be effectively reversed, as in "You've done nothing but complain ever since you got here." The punch line is clear to the audience once the word "complain" is uttered, yet the audience must wait for the rest of the sentence to be completed before laughing - a clear violation of the law of deflation.

EXAMPLE #71: THE LAW OF CARICATURE

The woman in this hilarious anecdote should be portrayed as hysterical when the punch line is delivered. But be sure to exaggerate your features and vocal inflection until you have created a mockery of hysteria, not the real thing.

A woman was horrified one day to see her Doberman Pincer in the back yard clutching in his mouth the dead body of her neighbor's pet rabbit. Now, she and the neighbor lady didn't get along very well, and fearing the woman's wrath, she concocted a plan. She put the dead rabbit in the kitchen sink and scrubbed it clean. Then she fluffed up the fur and blow-dried it. She even tied a pretty bow around its neck, and then went and propped it up in its cage next-door. A few hours later, she heard the neighbor lady scream and saw her running across the lawn towards her. The lady was hysterical. The first lady, pretending not to know, asked, "What's wrong?" The neighbor through her tears said, "My rabbit. My rabbit!" The first lady said, "Calm down and tell me what's wrong." The lady tried to compose herself as she blurted out: "My precious rabbit! Three days ago he died and we buried him. AND HE'S BACK!"

There are few things, I suspect, that would be as earth-shattering to any of us as a real resurrection. But every Easter, we find life's greatest hope in that lady's words: "THREE DAYS AGO HE DIED AND WE BURIED HIM. (Pause briefly) AND HE'S BACK!"

EXAMPLE #72: THE LAW OF CARICATURE

The next two stories caricature the emotion of exasperation. The punch line of the first should be delivered as though the wife is not only exasperated, but speaking through her tears. Be sure to exaggerate her crying to cartoonish proportions, similar to the manner in which Wilma Flintstone cries in the cartoons. Her tears are humorous, not moving, and this is the critical issue. Authenticity is *definitely* not the desired objective.

64

A businessman was sitting in his office one day feeling guilty that he rarely treated his wife the way she deserved. So he took off work an hour early, stopped to buy a dozen roses and a box of candy, and went home. When he got there, he rang the front doorbell, and when his wife answered the door, he reached out and kissed her passionately. Then he handed her the flowers and candy and told her how much he loved her. To his shock, she burst into tears hysterically. He couldn't believe it. He said, "Honey, what's wrong?" She tried to compose herself, and said, "Oh, this has been the worst day of my life! First the kids were too sick to go to school, the baby's been crying all day long, the freezer broke down and thawed out sixty dollars worth of meat, and now..... [pause] NOW YOU'VE COME HOME DRUNK!"

Men, I wonder how many of your wives, if you showed up at the door with flowers and candy would conclude that you were drunk.

EXAMPLE #73: THE LAW OF CARICATURE

God's exasperation with the supplicant in this joke should not be expressed as sorrowful, but with a hint of demanding and impatience.

A man regularly got on his knees to beg God for a break in his paltry life. He prayed, "God, I've been good. I've tried to be kind. So please give me a break. Let me win the lottery!" He lost. The next month he prayed again, "Lord, please give me a break! Let me win the lottery." He lost again. The next month he prayed once more, "Lord, please let me win the lottery! Give me a break!" This time, God was fed up. In a booming voice from heaven he replied, "Give me a break! BUY A TICKET!"

There are a lot of desires that people have, but there is no hope that they'll ever come true, because they've never bought a ticket. What is the ticket you have to buy in order to place yourself in a position to achieve your goals?

EXAMPLE #74: THE LAW OF CARICATURE

Think for a moment about how Jerry Lewis or Jim Carrey would express the emotion of fear in one of their movies. Now contrast that expression with those of the characters in *Jurassic Park* when faced with a tyrannosaurus rex. Both are expressions of fear, yet one evokes laughter, the other terror. It is, of course, the former type of facial expression, voice inflection, and manner that the joke-teller strives to imitate.

A man decided to take his first skydive. He went through the training, and as he jumped from the plane he pulled the rip cord as he had been told to do. But nothing happened. Calmly applying his training, he reached for the emergency chute, and the cord came off in his hand. No parachute. Now panicked, he frantically tried to open the chute. That's when he noticed a man flying up from the earth towards him. He had no idea how the man was doing this, but he decided to take advantage of the opportunity. He shouted down to the approaching man, "Do you know anything about parachutes?" As they passed, the other man shouted back, "No! DO YOU KNOW ANYTHING ABOUT GAS STOVES?"

Now these guys had a problem. They had important questions, but no answers. We all find ourselves in those types of situations in our lives, don't we?

EXAMPLE #75: THE LAW OF CARICATURE

This story capitalizes on a sense of desperation on the part of two hunters.

Two men were out hunting, when they became hopelessly lost. Hours of yelling for help produced no results. Finally, one of them said, "In Boy Scouts they taught us that if we ever got lost, we should fire three shots into the air, and people will come find us." They tried it, firing three shots into the air in rapid succession. They did so every few minutes for six hours. Finally, one said to the other, "What should we do now?" The other one replied in anguish, "I don't know, it's almost dark [pause] AND WE'RE RUNNING OUT OF ARROWS!"

These guys had a problem. They were going through the motions of an activity they didn't fully understand. I'll bet you have several employees in your company that are having a similar struggle.

EXAMPLE #76: THE LAW OF CARICATURE

The punch line of this next story should be delivered with absolute incredulity. The previous line by the mourner should be delivered through cartoonish tears, which mix with disbelief only on the last line.

One of the world's richest men died, and at his funeral there was a great crowd. One particular man was weeping more loudly and profusely than anyone else. The funeral director walked over and tenderly put his hand on the man's shoulder. "Are you a relative of the deceased?" he asked. Through his tears, the man said, "No." The funeral director asked, "Then why are you crying?" The man looked up from his tears incredulously and snapped back, "BECAUSE I'M NOT A RELATIVE OF THE DECEASED!"

This guy had a problem. Money to him was more important than people. And when money becomes more important to you than people, you wind up losing both.

EXAMPLE #77: THE LAW OF CARICATURE

Three examples are provided here to demonstrate how even anger can be made humorous.

There was once a young man who appeared before a manager for a job interview. The manager asked what his qualifications were, to which the interviewee replied, "I have an MBA from Harvard Business School." The manager said, "That's good, what salary range are you expecting?" The young man replied: "At least $70,000 per year to start, with lots of perks." The manager raised an eyebrow, and asked, "And just what do you expect to do for all of that money?" The young graduate snapped back: "Absolutely nothing. I want to sit at a big desk shuffling papers for a couple of hours a day, and then go play golf." The manager had heard enough. He grabbed that kid by the scruff of the neck and bodily threw him out the front door. A fellow manager saw this spectacle unfold and walked up to his colleague. He said, "What in the world could that kid have done to make you so mad?" The interviewer said, "You wouldn't believe the nerve of that kid. He had the gall to come in here with no experience at all... AND APPLY FOR MY JOB!"

It's really easy to see our own faults in other people isn't it?

EXAMPLE #78: THE LAW OF CARICATURE

A patient in a mental ward claimed constantly that he was Napoleon. This really irritated his roommate, who said, "You idiot, don't you realize that if you would just quit saying you're Napoleon they would let you out of here?" The guy replied, "But I am Napoleon." "How do you know?" his roommate asked. The guy said, "Because God told me I'm Napoleon." The roommate angrily snapped back, "I NEVER SAID ANY SUCH THING!"

Of all the crazy notions circulating in corporate America today, I think that none could be crazier than the new age idea that we are gods.

EXAMPLE #79: THE LAW OF CARICATURE

A raw army recruit was assigned to a paratroop squad, and took his first lesson in skydiving. But he mistook the bomb-bay doors for the rest room, and stepped out of the airplane. His sergeant shouted after him: "Pull the cord on your left and the chute will open. There will be a truck on the ground waiting for you!" The young man pulled the cord, but the chute didn't open. He got mad. He said aloud, while hurtling toward the ground: "Doggonit! And I'll just bet THERE WON'T BE A TRUCK WAITING DOWN THERE EITHER!"

This man was suffering from a very common problem called denial. It's looking a problem square in the face and not recognizing its seriousness.

EXAMPLE #80: THE LAW OF CARICATURE

Try telling the punch line of this joke with a sense of mock horror and shock.

A man and his wife were arguing about what career would be appropriate for their teenage son. In order to settle the dispute, they agreed to a test. They put three items on the coffee table: a Bible, a ten dollar bill, and a bottle of whiskey. They reasoned that when the boy came in, if he picked up the Bible, he would be a preacher; if he picked up the ten spot, he would become a banker; and if he picked up the whiskey bottle, he would be a drunken bum all his life. They heard the boy walking up the front steps, so they hid behind the sofa to watch. The boy walked in, saw the items, and went over to the table. He rubbed his hand over the cover of the Bible thoughtfully. He turned the ten dollar bill over several times, studying it deeply. Then he fondled the cork on the whiskey bottle, removed it, and smelled it. Suddenly, a light came on in his eyes. He grabbed the ten dollar bill and shoved it in his pocket, tucked the Bible under his arm, and walked off drinking the whiskey. The parents watched with stupefied horror. Finally, when the boy was out of earshot, the man said aloud what both he and his wife had already concluded: "My God, Martha! HE'S GOING TO BE A POLITICIAN!"

Politics is a strange business, isn't it? It seems that the very thing people want in their leaders - integrity - would actually keep a person out of office. Something needs to change.

EXAMPLE #81: THE LAW OF CARICATURE

The policeman in this next yarn exudes a sense of getting in over his head, which grows until he finally blurts out the punch line with absolute anguish.

The story goes that the Pope was in America for one of his tours, and as he was being driven from one city to the next, he noticed that his chauffeur was wheezing and coughing, obviously suffering from a bad cold. Being the compassionate man that he is, the Pope offered to drive so that the chauffeur could get in the back seat and rest. Well, that's what they did. They got out on the open highway, but the Pope was unfamiliar with American cars and traffic laws, and before long he saw a patrolman's lights flashing behind him. He pulled over and watched in the mirror as the officer got out of his car and walked up to the limousine. The Pope rolled down the window, and the officer took one look at him and turned white as a sheet. He told the Pope to stay right there, hurriedly excused himself, and ran back to the patrol car. He radioed his sergeant and said, "Sarge, we've got a big problem. Guess who I just pulled to give a ticket!" The Sergeant said, "Who is it, a City Councilman?" The officer said, "No, he's more important than that." "You don't mean that you stopped the Mayor's car do you?" the sergeant asked. "No," the officer replied, obviously terrified, "He's lot's more important than that." "The Governor?" "No, he's more important than that." "The President of the United States?" "No, he's even more important than that." Now completely baffled, the Sergeant asked, "Well who in the world is it?" The frantic police officer blurted out: "I have no idea who he is, (pause) BUT HE'S GOT THE POPE FOR A CHAUFFEUR!"

How do you determine who is really important in the world? Is it being in the back seat of a limousine? Having lots of money? Being famous? No, I think the key to significance lies in...

EXAMPLE #82: THE LAW OF CARICATURE

The next joke features a caricature of defensiveness. The psychiatric patient should be characterized as incensed and defensive.

A man named Jones went to his psychologist to be analyzed, and the counselor immediately began to administer the Rorschach Ink Blot Test. He held up the first blot, which looks something like a fox who's been chasing parked cars. He said, "What do you see?" The patient said: "That's a picture of two people making love."

69

The psychologist raised an eyebrow. He held up the second blot, which resembles a couple of people playing patty-cake, and said, "What does this one look like?" The patient said, "It's a picture of two people making love." The therapist began to suspect he was onto something. He held up the third blot just to be sure. Now, the third blot looks like two people roasting a large butterfly over a camp fire. But the psychologist handed it to the man and asked, "And what do you make of this one?" The patient rolled his eyes and said exasperatedly: "It's a picture of two people making love!" The psychologist had heard enough. He said, "Mr. Jones, I believe that you have an obsession with sex." Jones was incensed! He couldn't believe what he was hearing. He said, "Me?!? I'm obsessed with sex?!? YOU'RE THE ONE WITH ALL THE DIRTY PICTURES!"

Now, Jones was in trouble. He had a problem, but he had convinced himself that the problem was not his, but someone else's. We all have a tendency to do that.

EXAMPLE #83: THE LAW OF CARICATURE

In order to summarize all of the laws discussed thus far, examine this wonderful piece of humor.

The story goes that an eccentric Texas Oil millionaire decided to throw a barbecue for about four thousand of his closest friends. After dinner, he had all the guests gather around his Olympic-sized swimming pool. He pulled the cover off of it, revealing about a dozen man-eating sharks. The crowd gasped. The millionaire said: "I have a challenge for you. To any man in this crowd who will dare to swim from one end of this pool to the other, I will give his choice of half of my oil wells, one million dollars, or the hand of my lovely daughter Bonnie-Lou in marriage." As soon as the words left his mouth, a man hit the surface of the pool and swam for all his might. A few seconds later he emerged from the far end of the pool gasping for breath. The millionaire was stunned. He said, "Son, I must admit, that I didn't think anyone would be brave enough to accept my challenge. But I am a man of my word. Which do you want: half of my oil wells, a million dollars, or the hand of my lovely daughter Bonnie-Lou in marriage?" "I don't want any of those things," the man snapped, still out of breath. The millionaire said, "Then what do you want?" The man looked around and said, "All I want is FIVE MINUTES ALONE WITH THE GUY WHO PUSHED ME IN THE POOL!"

Now this man was able to swim like never before because he was motivated. And a primary factor that determines whether or not you get eaten by the sharks in your world is how motivated you are.

Take note in the previous story of the use of each of the eight laws unveiled thus far. First the joke must, as always, be told with abandon. Second, tension builds very nicely with the offer of three possible prizes. Third and fourth, by saying the heart of the punch line smoothly, quickly and with proper cues, you will produce a very powerful pop of the comedy balloon. Fifth, notice that exaggeration is employed as the Texas oil millionaire hosted a party for four thousand of his closest friends. Sixth, personality has been added to the daughter by naming her Bonnie Lou. Seventh, the use of an outrageous Texas drawl (similar to that of the Looney Tunes character, Foghorn Leghorn, the rooster) will greatly enhance the humor of the story. And finally, the punch line must be delivered with a caricature of anger.

LAW NINE

The Law of Concealment

When listeners figure out a punch line before it is delivered, the joke is dead, no matter how funny it might otherwise be. For this reason, it is important to give the audience no hints at all about the outcome. Inexperienced joke tellers will find irresistible the temptation to add plausibility to a punch line by preceding it with unnecessary details. Such details allow some in the audience to anticipate the outcome, with the result that tension is gradually released throughout the joke instead of suddenly at its end. And of course, the balloon fizzles slowly into a limp pile of over-stretched rubber. It is far better to conceal such details than to try to lend credibility to the punch line by adding unnecessary information.

EXAMPLE #84: THE LAW OF CONCEALMENT

Following is a hysterical story about an elderly couple being taken on a stunt ride in a plane. At the end of the joke we discover that the old woman has fallen out of the plane. The first time I told this story, I felt compelled (because I already knew the outcome) to explain that this was the type of plane that had an open cockpit. As a result, half the audience figured out what was going to happen before I could finish the story. I should have been arrested for murdering a good joke!

A elderly couple decided to do something daring, so they stopped by a small airport and asked a pilot how much he would charge them to take them up for a flight. The man replied that he could do it for a hundred dollars. "A hundred dollars?!?" the octogenarian said. "I'll give you twenty." Well, they dickered back and forth, failing to come close to an agreeable price. Finally, the pilot said, "Look, I'll make you a deal. I'll take you both up. If you can get through the entire flight without making a sound, the trip is free. But if you make even a single noise, you pay the full one hundred dollars." The man said, "Deal." So they climbed in the tiny plane and the pilot took them on a dizzying ride with steep climbs, dives and barrel rolls, but not a peep was heard from the passengers. Finally, the pilot gave up and landed. They got out of the plane, and the pilot said, "Well, I really didn't think you could do it, but I'm a man of my word. The flight was free." Not one to gloat, the old man said, "Well, I have to admit there was one time when you almost had me." "Really?" the pilot said, "When was that?" The old man said, "WHEN MY WIFE FELL OUT."

Now, here's a man that had his priorities all fouled up. He cared more about a hundred bucks than he did his wife. But as silly as that story is, I'll bet there are some of you that are putting material things before your families, too.

EXAMPLE #85: THE LAW OF CONCEALMENT

As you spin this next yarn, resist the temptation to explain that the photographer didn't ask if he was boarding the correct plane. Let the audience figure this out after the punch line.

When a huge fire broke out in the Rocky Mountains, a photographer from the local newspaper was dispatched to get some pictures of it. However, firemen had barricaded the roads and refused to let anyone in. Undaunted, the photographer called the local airport and hired a pilot to fly him over the fire. When he arrived, the plane was sitting on the tarmac ready to go, so the photographer jumped in and said, "Let's go." He directed the pilot to fly as close to the fire as he could to provide the best possible photo opportunities. The pilot repeatedly maneuvered the plane through the dense smoke, perilously close to the flames, as he had been requested to do. As they returned to the airport, the pilot asked, "What are you taking all of those pictures for?" The man replied, "It's my job. I work for the newspaper." There was silence for a few moments, after which the pilot asked, "You mean, YOU'RE NOT THE FLIGHT INSTRUCTOR?"

These guys had a problem. Both of them got into a difficult position, each assuming the other knew how to handle it. I can't think of a better illustration of why marriages fail so often. Two young people fly into the fire, each assuming they have what it takes between them to get themselves out of it.

EXAMPLE #86: THE LAW OF CONCEALMENT

Experienced comedians will know not to reveal before the punch line of this story that one brother was even worse than the other. The punch line should be the first hint of this fact that the audience hears.

There was once a rural church which had among its members two elderly men - twin brothers - who were just as mean and rotten as they could be. The minister always secretly hoped that he would move to another church before either of them died because he knew there was not a single good thing he could say in a funeral about either one of them. No such luck. One of the men did die, and as the pastor was wrestling with what to say at the funeral, the surviving twin walked into his office. He said, "Pastor, I know that my brother was a wicked man. But I hope that you can say some good words about him in the funeral. In fact, if you will say just once that he was a saint, the family will show it's gratitude by donating $50,000 from his estate to the church." Well, if the minister hadn't been in a quandary before, now he was certainly in one. He just couldn't decide what to do. The day of the funeral arrived, and the Minister strode to the pulpit, still wrestling with his dilemma. Then suddenly, as though the waters had parted, he knew what he must do. He could not tell a lie. He started: "Friends, we all know that the dear departed was a wicked man. He drank way too much. He cheated on his wife, Hildegard, all the time. He was a lazy, no-count bum and a liar from boyhood. [Pause.] BUT COMPARED TO HIS BROTHER, HE WAS A SAINT!"

Now, this preacher was a problem-solver.

EXAMPLE #87: THE LAW OF CONCEALMENT

Resist the temptation in this next story to tell your listeners that when the men crawled out of the plane that they were surrounded by wreckage.

The story goes that two hunters hired a pilot to fly them out to a remote forest where they could hunt moose. The pilot dropped them off, and was told to pick up the hunters at that same spot two weeks later. Sure enough, a fortnight later the pilot returned, but to his surprise, the two hunters had between them shot three moose. The pilot freaked! He said, "Look, there's no way my little plane can take the weight of the three of us plus three moose!" Well, now the hunters were miffed. They said, "Wait just a minute, buddy! Every year we fly to this spot, every year we shoot three moose, and the pilot has just tied them on top of the plane, and their planes were no bigger than yours." Well, the pilot couldn't argue with experience, so he shrugged and said, "Okay." He lashed those three moose on top of the plane, and took off down the runway. It seemed like forever, but the plane finally left the ground. It just barely cleared the treetops. It shimmied and creaked and groaned for about twenty miles, before finally crashing into the side of a mountain. The three men crawled out of the wreckage, brushed themselves off, and looked around. The pilot said, "I don't suppose either of you knows where we are?" One of the hunters sighed and said: "Yeah. SAME PLACE WE CRASH EVERY YEAR!"

Now these guys crashed in the same place over and over because they didn't learn from their past failures.

EXAMPLE #88: THE LAW OF CONCEALMENT

Sometimes the punch line unavoidably becomes obvious during the sentence that precedes it. A race thus ensues between the mouth of the storyteller and the minds of the hearers. The critical issue becomes this: can you finish telling the story before the audience figures it out for themselves? For this reason, it is essential in such cases that there be no hesitation at all before delivering the remainder of the joke. Otherwise, the tension in the balloon will be dissipated before you can finish the story. For instance, in the following bit of funniness, most of your audience will discern that the answer to the counselor's question will reflect a misunderstanding in the mind of the husband related to who does the kissing. Consequently, you must allow not even a second of silence before the punch line. Instead, you must continue to talk rapidly so that the audience will have no time to anticipate the outcome.

A couple went to a psychologist for marriage counseling. After listening for a while, the counselor said, "I know what the problem is." He walked over to the wife, took her in his arms, and kissed her passionately. The woman was dazed, but delighted. The doctor turned to the husband and said, "Your wife needs that kind of treatment at least three times per week." The man said, "O.K. I'LL BRING HER IN ON MONDAYS, WEDNESDAYS, AND FRIDAYS."

The thing that makes that story so funny is the fact that it is so typical of the way men think. We (they) just don't understand romance.

EXAMPLE #89: THE LAW OF CONCEALMENT

A similar weakness exists in this story involving a cowboy and a religious horse. Be aware that the moment the horse skids to a stop on the edge of a canyon, the audience will figure out that the cowboy's next words will be his last. Hence, it is essential that the punch line be delivered immediately on the heels of the preceding sentence.

An old cowpoke was looking to buy himself a horse, and called on a rancher who had advertised that he had one for sale. The horse was beautiful, and the cowboy asked if he could take her for a test ride. The owner replied that he could, but he needed to learn a whole new set of commands, because this horse had been trained by his wife, who was a very religious person. He said, "For example, if you want to make this horse gallop, you say 'Thank You Lord.' If you want him to stop, you say 'Amen.'" The cowboy reckoned he could handle that. "Thank You Lord," he shouted, and the horse took off like a filly at the Kentucky Derby. He was riding like the wind when he suddenly realized that he could no longer remember the "stop" command. He shouted "Whoooaaa," but the horse kept galloping. He tried every spiritual saying he could think of, and became more frantic as he saw that the horse was galloping toward a canyon. "Hallelujah!" he shouted. "Take an offering!" "Sunday School!" Finally, he remembered and shouted, "Amen!" and the horse skidded to a stop on the rim of the canyon. THE GRATEFUL COWBOY LOOKED HEAVEN-WARD AND SAID: "THANK YOU LORD!"

This cowboy learned the hard way that the words you say can save you or kill you.

LAW TEN

The Law of Preparation

Some jokes simply will not stand alone. That is, to tell such a story without providing a context in which to easily understand the punch line will prove to be a waste of a perfectly good joke. For instance, this next example is about Moses receiving Ten Commandments from God, (not just one) because they were free. If told without preparing the listeners in advance, the joke makes little sense, or it takes so long to figure out that the tension dissipates slowly. The punch line ("They're free? Then I'll take ten!") will not puncture the balloon at all unless you have already mentioned that Jewish people are renowned for their ability to spot a bargain. Before telling a joke, be sure that you have asked yourself whether it needs to be set-up in advance.

EXAMPLE 90: THE LAW OF PREPARATION

Perhaps you've wondered just how the Ten Commandments came to be. Well, God was looking for someone to whom He could deliver a message. There was nomad wandering through the desert of Sinaii one day when God spoke to him from heaven. The Lord said, "Hey, I've got a commandment for you." "How much does it cost?" the guy asked. "It's free," God said. "Well what is it?" the guy asked. The Lord answered: "Thou shalt not steal." Immediately the man said, "No way, Lord. I'm with a band of marauding thieves, and I make my living by stealing. So I can't take one." A little later, the caravan of an Arabian sheik happened by. God said to the sheik: "I have a commandment for you." "How much does it cost?" the sheik inquired. "It's free," God assured him. Potentially interested, the sheik asked, "Well, what is it?" The Lord answered, "Thou shalt not commit adultery." Immediately the sheik said, "No way, Lord. I've got dozens of wives and concubines. I can't be limited to just one woman, so I just can't take a commandment right now." Not long after, the great Jewish leader Moses came by. God said, "I've got a commandment for you." Moses said, "How much does it cost?" God said, "It's free." Moses snapped back, "THEN I'LL TAKE TEN."

Well, like Moses, I'm always looking for a bargain.

EXAMPLE 91: THE LAW OF PREPARATION

Prepare your audience for this next story by mentioning that marriage is difficult, or that young husbands tend to be very insensitive, or that divorce is too easy in our culture, etc.

In the old west, a cowboy and his young bride had just gotten married, and immediately headed off in a horse-drawn carriage toward town for their honeymoon. Suddenly, a rabbit darted across the road and startled the horse, who bolted. The new husband quietly dismounted, walked up to the horse, looked him square in the eye, and said, "That's number one." The bride thought this was very curious, but said nothing. They continued down the road, and the horse stumbled slightly. Again, the man walked to the front of the horse and said, "That's number two." They continued down the road, which passed through a creek, and the horse stopped for a drink. The man stepped down into the water, walked up to the horse and said: "That's number three." With that, he took out his revolver and shot the horse dead. The woman couldn't believe it. She said, "You idiot what are you doing? That's our only horse?" The man quietly looked back at his wife and responded, "THAT'S NUMBER ONE."

In ancient Rome, a man could divorce his wife legally by just saying "I divorce you" three times. It was a "three strikes and your out" mentality. But Jesus taught that we are to forgive seventy times seven times. Who's right?

EXAMPLE 92: THE LAW OF PREPARATION

A necessary set-up for this narrative about a trip to heaven is mention of the concept that what we give away on earth is stored up for us in heaven. Telling this very funny story without preparing the audience in this way will cause it to fail miserably.

A millionaire died and appeared before the pearly gates. St. Peter ushered him in and offered to take him to his eternal dwelling. As they walked, the man was astounded by the beauty and size of the mansions. He passed rows of spectacular homes too beautiful to describe. Knowing that the residents of those homes could not possibly have been as wealthy as he, he could only imagine the grandeur of the home that awaited him. Finally, St. Pete stopped in front of a grass hut and said, "That's yours." Immediately the millionaire began to object and complain. He said, "How could you stick me in such a hovel as this?" St. Peter put up his hand and said: "I don't want to hear it. You have no right to complain. WE DID THE BEST WE COULD WITH WHAT YOU SENT US!"

They say you can't take it with you. If that's true, it's all the more important that you send it ahead. You do that by giving it away.

EXAMPLE 93: THE LAW OF PREPARATION

Set this next joke up by talking about the rampant political corruption in our society.

A wealthy and powerful man was lying on his deathbed, and called to his side two U.S. Congressmen whom he had supported heavily in their election campaigns. They came to the hospital and sat on either side of him as he waited to die. While each politician was willing to participate in the vigil, they couldn't help but be curious as to why the old man had chosen them to come to his bedside. So they asked him why. The old man said, "Well, it's like this: I WANTED TO DIE LIKE JESUS DID BETWEEN TWO THIEVES."

It sure seems like some of the people we've sent to Washington are thieves doesn't it?

EXAMPLE 94: THE LAW OF PREPARATION

An appropriate way to prepare the listeners for this story is to state that men sometimes tend to get their priorities misplaced, or that men are too concerned about sports to put their families first.

It was Superbowl Sunday, and the stadium was packed to capacity. In fact, there was only one empty seat in the entire stadium - right next to a lonely looking man. A nearby spectator couldn't help but ask why the seat was empty. The man replied: "I bought these tickets over six months ago. This one was for my wife, but she died." The spectator said, "I'm so sorry to hear that, but couldn't you have at least given the ticket to a friend or relative?" The man shook his head and said, "No. THEY'RE ALL AT THE FUNERAL."

Priorities are a really hard thing to get a grip on in life aren't they? How are you supposed to make those difficult choices between family, work and leisure?

EXAMPLE 95: THE LAW OF PREPARATION

The most effective preparation for this next example is the mention that some people are cheapskates or are always looking for an opportunity to scam someone.

There was once an elderly man who went on vacation in another state. While he was there, he began to feel ill, so he went through the yellow pages and found a nearby doctor. He went to the clinic, signed in, and as he was sitting in the waiting room he noticed a sign that said: "First visit, $50.00; Every visit thereafter, $25.00." Well, eventually he was taken to an examining room, and the doctor came in to see him. The man shook the doctor's hand and said, "It's good to see you again." The doctor looked puzzled but replied, "It's good to see you again, too." The doctor asked, "What seems to be your problem?" Continuing his ruse, the man said, "Oh, same as last time. My stomach hurts, my joints are achy, and I can't sleep nights. What should I do, Doc?" The doctor turned to leave and on his way out the door, he said, "JUST KEEP DOING WHAT I TOLD YOU TO DO LAST TIME!"

We have a term in the English language to describe what happened to this old man who wanted to swindle this doctor out of 25 bucks, but wound up hoodwinked out of 25, himself. We call it "poetic justice," and it always works. That's why there's no substitute for plain old integrity.

EXAMPLE 96: THE LAW OF PREPARATION

The next three jokes all center on the church, and should be set up by mentioning that churches are sometimes too spiritually minded, too self-right-eous, and too unfocused, respectively.

A Sunday School teacher was becoming a little discouraged with the response of his fourth-grade boys' class. They seemed bored. So he decided to start his next lesson with a riddle, thinking that this would surely gain their interest. So he stood up in front of the class and said: "Okay, boys, what's gray, has a bushy tail, and eats nuts?" To his surprise, he was met with complete silence. He tried again: "Come on boys, what's gray, has a bushy tail, and eats nuts?" Still no answer. He turned to his star pupil and said, "Bobby, surely you know the answer. What's gray, has a bushy tail, and eats nuts?" Bobby squirmed in his seat and finally said reluctantly, "Well, it sounds like a squirrel to me, but... I'LL SAY GOD."

You know, some people can get so heavenly minded that they are no earthly good. They're always looking for spiritual answers to questions that can be easily answered much more practically.

EXAMPLE 97: THE LAW OF PREPARATION

A man died and was escorted through heaven by Saint Peter, himself. He showed him the Baptist, then the Methodist, then the Catholic section of heaven. Then they came to a huge wall with a sign on it that said: "Presbyterians." [Use whatever denomination you want to pick on here.] The man looked through a crack in the wall and saw a huge throng of people. He said to St. Pete: "Hey, why are the Presbyterians behind this wall?" Peter quickly said, "Shhhh! Don't let them hear you. THEY THINK THEY'RE THE ONLY ONES HERE!"

The self-righteousness of some religious people is appalling, isn't it?

EXAMPLE 98: THE LAW OF PREPARATION

Two men were stranded on a desert island after their boat sank. They had tried everything they knew to attract attention - signal fires, messages in bottles, writing "help" in the sand, but all to no avail. Finally, they decided that prayer was their only hope. One said to the other, "I've never been to church. I don't know how to pray, do you?" The other replied, "Well, I've never been to church either, but I grew up next door to a big Catholic church, and I overheard them praying all the time. I think I can do what they did." So the two men bowed their heads, and the one said, "B -14. I -12. N - 23."

I think that the church is failing to communicate to people outside what it really stands for.

EXAMPLE #99: THE LAW OF PREPARATION

Preface this story with a comment that life is hard sometimes, and it's tough to get motivated.

A mother went into her son's bedroom one morning to awaken him. She said, "Get up, Son, or you'll be late for school." He pulled the covers over his head and said, "No! I'm not going to school today!" When she asked him why, he replied, "Because none of the kids like me!" She said, "Well, you have to go anyway." He said, "Give me three good reasons." She responded, "Okay, I will. One: It's builds character when you can motivate yourself to do something that you don't want to do. Two: If you go today, maybe you'll find a student who likes you. And Three: YOU'RE 43 YEARS OLD AND YOU'RE THE PRINCIPAL!"

No matter now old or educated we may be, we all sometimes lose our motivation, don't we?

EXAMPLE #100: SUMMARY OF TEN LAWS

All ten laws described so far will greatly improve the following joke. Observe how a relatively tame joke can become a powerful tool in the hands of one who knows how to harness and use the immutable laws of humor in harmony with one another.

[Obey the Law of Preparation by first commenting that churches often place power in the hands of people who don't know what they're talking about.] A church committee was debating the viability of a proposal to purchase a new chandelier for the sanctuary. One old deacon named Elijah, [Use the Law of Personality to mimic a feisty old deacon's mannerisms.] who had been a member of the church for about a hundred and thirty years, [The Law of Exaggeration] represented the faction that opposed the purchase. He stood up to address the meeting. He said, [Use the Law of Inflection here, speaking with the dialect of an elderly Southerner.] "We are opposed to this purchase of the chandelier for three reasons. One: [Note that the Law of Inflation is being complied with by using three increasingly funny punch lines.] We can't order one BECAUSE NO ONE HERE KNOWS HOW TO SPELL IT. [Pause for a light chuckle from the audience.] Two: It's of no value BECAUSE NO ONE HERE KNOWS HOW TO PLAY IT. [Pause for laughter.] And three: [Go out on a limb and say this with Abandon. Also, say it with mock anger and authoritativeness, in cooperation with the Law of

Caricature.] If we've got extra money to spend, WHAT WE NEED IS SOME MORE LIGHT [On the word Light you should raise your eyebrows and turn raise your palm above waist level to prompt audience laughter.] IN HERE!" [Be sure to comply with the Law of Deflation by saying the punch line smoothly and quickly.]

The great problem with management by committee is the involvement of people who don't do their homework, and know nothing about which they speak, yet they still have the same voting power as those who do.

LAW ELEVEN

The Law of Rebounding

This is my favorite law, because it guarantees that you will never again tell a joke without getting a good laugh. How? If you tell a joke that absolutely bombs, you can "catch it on the rebound" and get an even bigger laugh *from your reaction to the fact that your joke bombed!* The David Letterman monologue provides an excellent example of this principle. Notice that when Letterman delivers a one-liner that gets no response from the audience, he responds in a funny way. He grimaces terribly, or he tears up the cue card, or he pretends to be mad at the audience, or he deadpans the failed punch line again. I have many times told jokes that bombed on stage. My response? I grimace, feign sheepishness, grab a piece of paper off my podium, ball it up and throw it away! The laughter I get from this stunt is almost always far greater than what I would have gotten from the joke if it had worked according to my plans.

LAW TWELVE

The Law of Proximity

People who are isolated - whether physically or emotionally - rarely laugh. Three factors produce this curious phenomenon. First, a person sitting in a room with several empty seats around him feels that he is "on display," and that laughing aloud will only make him seem more so. Consequently, when the isolated person hears a hilarious joke, he merely smiles, fearing that laughing aloud would call attention to himself, and embarrass him. To counteract this tendency, every seasoned speaker knows to have the audience members sit close together whenever possible.

Second, laughter is a relational thing. People who hear a funny story first laugh, then a moment later turn and make eye contact with the person/people they came with. If a person came alone, however, laughter seems somewhat inappropriate.

Third, when an audience is composed almost entirely of people who do not know one another, even if they are crammed together, they are reticent to laugh (unless they "feel" they know each other already, due to a common occupation, problem, goal, etc.). This hesitancy to laugh exists because each person knows instinctively that after laughing, he or she is supposed to make eye contact with the person in the next chair. So if a person does not know those seated around him, he will often choose not to laugh, thus excusing himself from the awkwardness of making eye contact with a complete stranger. These factors can be overcome by "warming up" the audience by shaking hands with them, interacting with them, helping them meet those around them, etc.

So there you have it! Twelve unchanging laws that will enable you to get guaranteed laughs from any good joke, and a whole lot of bad ones as well!

THE END

About The Author

Relevant, insightful, and life-changing. Those words describe the motivational message of Billy Riggs. Billy has been speaking publicly for the last 20 years and has since delivered his message to more than two million people on five continents. After receiving his two master's degrees, he founded and pastored one of America's fastest growing churches, which grew from 0 to 2,000 in attendance in just three years.

Billy is also a world-class illusionist, who has performed his spectacular illusions on nine cruise ships and before audiences as large as 20,000. He currently travels full time speaking to businesses and associations about life's most crippling illusions. In addition to this book, *The Twelve Immutable Laws of Humor*, he has also produced nearly fifty different audio cassette albums.

For information on Billy's programs or to arrange for a presentation to your group as a keynote speaker, please contact:

Visions & Ventures, Inc.
3243 Swandale
San Antonio, TX 78230-4439

Voice: (800) 299-5591
Fax: (210) 341-4637
e-mail: agent@billyriggs.com

Audio Tapes By Billy Riggs

Grand Illusions

False perceptions of reality, most of them buried in the subconscious mind, constitute life's single greatest obstacle to achievement. Instilled in us by childhood experiences, these faulty assumptions reach from the past to paralyze potential. Such debilitating myths reduce would-be leaders to followers. Now, in a profound and inspiring message, life's three Grand Illusions℠ are exposed to the light of reality. This spellbinding presentation vanishes a lifetime of confusion..$10.00

Pay No Attention To That Man Behind the Curtain

Emotional exhaustion is the inevitable result of pretense. Driven by a single dominant emotion rooted in past experiences, virtually all adults wear masks chosen to protect them from their deepest fears. The strain of maintaining this protective facade sometimes proves unbearable, resulting in depression, coronary-artery disease, and nervous breakdown. Courage to remove the mask comes only when the hidden sources of one's fears are identified, exposed, and eliminated. The resulting freedom improves satisfaction, prevents burnout and raises productivity...$10.00

How To Drive Yourself, Without Driving Yourself Crazy

The inherent danger of passion-induced work is its appetite for consuming all of life. Whether motivated by obsession or necessity, the driven worker is in jeopardy of losing family, integrity, health and happiness. By internalizing the four core values of character, intimacy, achievement and reliance, you will harness the power of an integrated life and move beyond survival to success and balance. You will discover how to *"Drive Yourself Without Driving Yourself (or those around you) Crazy"*.................$10.00

How To Start an Epidemic... Without Becoming A Plague

Businesses, like bicycles, derive their stability from forward motion, so explosive and instantaneous growth will become essential to the survival of new projects and products in the fast-paced future. Such growth is the most feasible way to overcome "initial inertia." By formulating, nurturing, and communicating your dream, you can quickly achieve the total goal ownership necessary for immediate success in almost any endeavor. The **How To Start An Epidemic** system enables you to achieve immediate momentum through imaging, and maintain it by repeatedly painting the vision...$10.00

Order by calling **(800)203-0720**, or write to Billy Riggs; 3243 Swandale Street; San Antonio, TX 78230

VISA, MasterCard, and American Express accepted.